Major
Hans "Assi" Hahn

The Man
And His Machines

Major Hans "Assi" Hahn
The Man and His Machines

by

Jerry Crandall

Illustrated by Thomas A. Tullis

ISBN 0-9721060-0-6
Library of Congress Catalog Number: 2002094873

First Edition

Printed in Korea

Library of Eagles

Eagle Editions Ltd.
Post Office Box 580
Hamilton MT 59840 USA
www.eagle-editions.com

We are interested in hearing from those who may have photographic or data material for use in future publications

Contents

Dedicated
with love to the wonderful

Gisela Hahn

for her support, cooperation and blessings.
I understand why Assi was so fascinated by this multi-talented lady.

Acknowledgements

This project came about after meeting *Frau* Gisela Hahn, Assi Hahn's widow and Wolfgang Falck in 1987, first at the *Jagdgeschwader* 2 *"Richthofen"* reunion held in Nidda, Germany, then at their home in the Austrian Alps. These warm, wonderful people capture the heart of anyone they meet, especially mine. Gisela's boundless enthusiasm and willingness to share her photos, stories and documents of her late husband was the driving force behind this story.

Every year since then my wife Judy and I have had the privilege of visiting Gisela and Wolf, growing to love and respect them as our dearest family members. Wolfgang Falck has been a beacon of support supplying insight about his late friend Assi Hahn. Many people have given their support and I extend my deepest appreciation and heartfelt thanks to them all:

	Gisela Hahn	**Wolfgang Falck**
Julius Meimberg	**Erich Hartmann +**	**Diethelm von Eichel-Streiber +**

Bernd Barbas, John Beaman, Christer Bergström, Douglas Champlin, Arno Dill, Russell Fahey, Jean-Bernard Frappe, Carl Geust, Marne Hrabak, Helga Hosford, PhD., Heinz Jirousek, Viktor Kulikov, Jean-Yves Lorant, Richard Lutz, Walter Matthiesen, Kai Müller-Leibenau, Bill and Diana Neaves, Werner Oeltjebruns, Jim Perry, Peter Petrick, Gennadiy Petrov, Hans Ring, Col. Ray Toliver (ret), Robert Venema, David Wadman and Bernd Willmer. My humblest apologies to anyone I may have overlooked.

Thanks to Carl and Doris Charles for assistance during a challenging time.

Much appreciation to Jan Bobek and the first-rate magazine **Revi** of the Czech Republic.

A special acknowledgement of thanks to Kent Haaven of *Images* for his design work.

And to my wife Judy for all of her work above and beyond the call of duty.

Major Hans "Assi" Hahn

"Assi Hahn as a person was a man with absolutely the greatest influence on human beings that I ever knew. As young students in Germany at the *Kriegsschule* (War College) in München we were in the same classroom with the same company of about 100 young officer candidates. He was excellent, had a fabulous memory and a great ability to comprehend any situation.

"Even his officers had such respect for him; for example every morning we had to take a cold shower but Assi didn't like it so he didn't go everyday. When the duty officer was checking the rooms they would open the door and see him lying in bed. Quickly the duty officer would close the door pretending not to have seen Assi lying there!

"Simply through mimicking, Assi had the ability to make someone look ridiculous once and for all and everybody knew it. He wouldn't do anything else than what he felt but he was an excellent soldier and the teachers figured that in his case they would just let that go through. He was a born leader and he showed it. Assi looked totally different from everybody else possessing a strong face and extremely expressive mouth. Even as a young man, for we were boys at that time, 21 or 22, Assi already had a powerful personality. At that age you are still much more a boy than a man, but he was!

"Everything he did had to be planned. Automatically, whenever something was going on that required a leader, Assi would be it. He had a tremendous eye, and was very quick in his decision process always making the right ones immediately. Later when we became fighter pilots, Assi was a natural. When we were together in St. Pol, France for example, even though I can't recall many details, I can tell you that when he was in the air, he always saw the British Spitfires first. I don't recall him ever loosing a plane while he was in the air with us. Assi was a leader who flew, not a guy who was sitting down on the ground sending the others up. He was the number one man in the plane."

Major **Diethelm von Eichel-Streiber**
10 August 1914 – 13 May 1996
Knight's Cross Recipient
96 Victories,
JG 52, JG 2, JG 77, JG 5, JG 26, JG 51, JG 27

Chapter One
Beginnings

Deep in the forested heartland area of Thuringen, Germany lies the city of Gotha, rich in medieval history. Nearby is the city of Eisenach, the birthplace of Johann Sebastian Bach, and where the religious leader Martin Luther crusaded for church reform.[1]

Born in Gotha to the family Hahn, father Arthur and mother Helene, on 14 April 1914, was Hans Robert Fritz Hahn. From his first days, his parents and older sister Käte had their hands full with young Hans. His personality traits developed at an early age. Being a practical joker, full of fun and laughter he also possessed a natural abil-

As a young man Assi was infatuated with all the arts, especially with theatre and movies. Note large portrait of Marlene Dietrich above Assi's head.

A young Assi with his older sister Käte, at their home in Gotha, Germany.

ity to learn and absorb new things. Friends altered his name "Hans" to "Hansi", ultimately becoming "Assi". And the name stuck. Although his parents still called him Hans, to the rest of the world, he became "Assi Hahn".

As he grew into manhood his strong personality forged his lifelong characteristics. He developed a love of the arts, paintings, poetry and a fascination for the movie stars of that period especially Marlene Dietrich. A natural athlete blessed with a powerful stocky build, Assi pursued skiing and other sports such as track and field. In fact he was selected to participate in the Eleventh Summer Olympic Games held in Berlin Germany, 1936, competing in the pentathlon event. Due to illness, however, he was forced to withdraw. All these qualities helped shape the foundation for the strenuous task ahead of air combat and leading fighter pilots into war.

Assi Hahn entered military service on 1 April 1934 as an officer candidate in the 14th Infantry Regiment, attending War College in München for about one year in 1935. In November 1935, Assi transferred into the *Luftwaffe* and started basic flight training at Celle, Germany. He received his officer's commission to *Leutnant* on 1

April 1936. His first assignment was to 4./JG 134, (II. *Gruppe*) *"Horst Wessel"* based in Western Germany at Werl near Dortmund. Here he flew the Arado Ar 65, 68 F biplanes and the early versions of the new Messerschmitt 109, first the B then the D-1 sub-types. His tour of duty here lasted from 15 April 1936 to 31 October 1937.

A new *Jagdfliegerschule* (fighter pilot's school) was formed at Werneuchen, Northeast of Berlin and Assi was promoted to Flight Instructor and Company Leader of 1. *Staffel,* a position he held until 1 April 1938.

Above; **Leutnant** *Hahn on the right in front of one of the Arado 68 Fs he flew in 4./JG 134 "Horst Wessel" from 15 April 1936 to 31 October 1937. This machine was "White 4". Of interest is the assigned unit color Brown with narrow trim on the fuselage and the Red circle in the fuel triangle.*

Assi on the right with unidentified pilot in front of "White 4", W. Nr. 1588.

Lt. Hahn on the right in front of "White 4", Arado 68 F of 4./JG 134 "Horst Wessel".

"White 12" Arado 68 F of 4./JG 134 with Lt. Hahn at the controls. Photo taken 22 May 1937.

Hans Hahn
Leutnant im Jagdgeschwader „Horst Wessel"

Business card of Lt. Hans Han.

Right: Lt. Hahn in "White 12".

Recognized for his outstanding leadership ability he was prematurely promoted to *Oberleutnant* on 1 February 1939. The next assignment for Assi Hahn was to the *Stab* [staff] of I./JG 3 *"Udet"* based at Merseburg, Germany.

*Right; Business card for Assi while at **Jagdfliegerschule** Werneuchen.*

Hans Hahn
Leutnant und Kompanieführer

Jagdfliegerschule Werneuchen

*Assi Hahn's class photo of **Jagdfliegerschule** (Fighter Pilot's School) Werneuchen, November 1937 to April 1938. Assi is wearing his officer's cap standing in the front row, fourth from the right with the dog.*

*Lt. Hahn, center, surrounded by his 1. **Staffel** at the **Jagdfliegerschule Werneuchen** in front of an early Bf 109 coded S2 + 54.*

Photos taken in September 1939 reveal his aircraft at this time was a Bf 109 E-3 with the appropriate single *Winkel* (chevron) for a *Stab* machine. Here for the first time, we see Assi's personal emblem of a rooster's head that appeared on both sides of the engine cowling. The name "Hahn" in the German language translates in English to "Rooster".

Interestingly there was another prominent pilot named Hans von Hahn who also used a roos-

ter head for his personal emblem and even more coincidently he came to I./JG 3 "*Udet*" as its *Kommandeur* on 27 August 1940, almost a year after Assi's departure from JG 3.

Later when Assi became III./JG 2 *Kommandeur*, he altered the rooster emblem into a streamlined design that decorated the engine cowlings of all III. *Gruppe* aircraft. The known photos of his II./JG 54 aircraft, Assi's last assignment, show no rooster emblem.

For a time, Assi served in the **Stab** *of I./JG 3 "Udet" stationed at Merseburg, Germany September 1939. This was his Bf 109 E-3 with the* **Stab** *chevron and his personal emblem of the rooster head. The name "Hahn" means "rooster". (Aircraft No. 1).*

Another Bf 109 E-3 of I./JG 3 with a personal marking of what appears to be a dragon.

Below: A sign forbidding anyone but I./JG 3 personnel to be in the area.

*Aircraft and equipment of I./JG 3. Major Otto-Heinrich von Houwald, the **Gruppen-kommandeur's** Bf 109 E is in front. The double chevron can just be seen under the protective tarp. The **Stab** machine of Assi Hahn is next, then two more aircraft of the I. Gruppe. A few days after this image was taken, early October 1939 at Merseberg, the original photo was processed at nearby Leipzig.*

Chapter 1 Notes:

1. Another prominent *Luftwaffe* fighter pilot, Hannes Trautloft also from this area. Born two years earlier than Assi Hahn, Trautloft became *Geschwaderkommodore* of the JG 54 Green Hearts, so named for the dark green forest heartland of this area. Eventually he became the *Luftwaffe's* Inspector of Day Fighters.

Chapter Two
Jagdgeschwader "Richthofen"

By order dated 11 October 1939, II. *Gruppe* JG 2 "*Richthofen*" was formed around a nucleus of personnel from I./JG 2 and I./JG 3. Departing from his post of *Stab* I./JG 3 Oblt. Hahn was promoted to *Staffelkapitän* of 4./JG 2 on 15 December 1939, based at Zerbst, Germany.

Oblt. Hahn led the 4. *Staffel* flying "White 13" Bf 109 E-3. In late February, 1940, the *Gruppe* moved to Nordholz, Germany. During the beginning phases of the battle of France the II. *Gruppe* moved to Münster, Germany then to several airfields in Belgium. Assi's first victory was during a battle over Gemblaux, Belgium, over a RAF Hurricane.[1]

Lt. Hahn with **Oberleutnant** *Werner Mölders, before Assi was awarded the Knight's Cross.*

Business card of Oblt. and **Staffelkapitän** *of 4./JG 2 Assi Hahn.*

Hans Hahn
Oberleutnant und Staffelkapitän
im Jagdgeschwader Richthofen

February 1940 taken at Nordholz, Northern Germany here Assi is suffering from a bad toothache. Assi was promoted to **Staffelkapitän** *on 15 December 1939.*

"White 2" 4. Staffel taken on January 1940 at Nordholz, Northern Germany.

Assi's "White 13" (Aircraft No. 2) taken in March 1940 at Nordholz, Northern Germany.

Assi's Bf 109 E-3 "White 13". Some late E-3 subtypes were equipped with the square canopy fitted to the E-4. Assi's first victory on 14 May was with this aircraft. (Aircraft No. 2)

A story published in the Zerbst *Stadtnachrichten* newspaper dated 6 September 1941 reports Hptm[2]. Hahn's first victory:

"I pressed the button...And the British Airplane burst into Flames...

'What is the story of your first victory?' we asked. *Hauptmann* Hahn told us about his first aerial combat. It was 14 May 1940. His *Geschwader* was located in Belgium at that time. The weather was hazy. Visibility was miserable. He flew with his *Staffel* north of Namur when two squadrons of Spitfires and Hurricanes suddenly appeared at 8000 meters altitude above Brussels. The Germans encountered the English fighters for the first time. Action was needed. 'I did what I had been taught

for years and what I had always beaten into my students: Go!

I approached the first British airplane to ten meters. Then I pressed the button hard, and the British airplane burst into flames, and the enemy crashed down with a long smoke plume. I immediately pulled my machine upward and got a Hurricane in sight, and it was only seconds when it too was done for.' The *Hauptmann* talks about this battle simply and unadorned as if there was nothing to it. These were the first two victories within the group, and when the machines flew home and announced their great success with wiggling their wings over their air base, the jubilation was general."

Assi Hahn, however did score a double victory on 19 May 1940 over a RAF Hurricane (second victory) and a French Morane 406 (third victory). His next two victories were also French, on 3 June a P-36 Hawk (fourth victory) and on 6 June another Morane 406 (fifth victory). His claimed victories recorded on the rudders of his aircraft reflected his first two claims on 10 May 1940 of 2 Hurricanes, but only one of these was officially recognized. As a result, the French victories for a long while were shown as his fourth, fifth and sixth victories, (see rudder photos of his Bf 109 F). This was corrected on the rudder of his Fw 190 A-2, W. Nr. 223 in May of 1942, now properly indicating his French victories as numbers 3, 4, and 5 as officially credited.

*In front of "White 13" are 4. **Staffel** pilots; L to R, Lt. Heinz Bolze, **Kapitän** Assi Hahn, Fw. Nels and Fw. Siegfried Schnell who was later awarded the Knight's Cross with Oak Leaves, killed on 25 February 1944 after achieving 93 victories.*

Below; "White 13" at Münster, Germany, April 1940, note JG 2 emblem has now been applied.

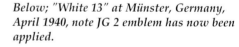

Above; Bf 109 E-3 "White 12" April 1940, Münster, Germany.

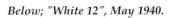

Below; "White 12", May 1940.

Lt. Krutein on Assi's pet donkey "Icko" in front of Hahn's "White 13". Photo taken in April 1940 at Münster, Germany.

Below; "White 8" Bf 109 E, 4./JG 2.

One member of the 4. *Staffel* that would be successful with 53 victories and be awarded the Knight's Cross was Lt. Julius "Jule" Meimberg.[3] Assi and Jule formed a life-long friendship. After Assi's death in December 1982, Meimberg remembered their first meeting[4]:

"In early winter 1939 Heinz Bolze, Egon Mayer and I were sent to Zerbst a small town near Magdeburg, Germany to the newly established II. *Gruppe* of *Jagdgeschwader 'Richthofen'*. We had just received our commissions to *Leutnant* and came right from the *Jagdflieger* school. After arrival in Zerbst, we were very tired as we spent the night on the train. The *Gruppenkommandeur* was Wolfgang Schellmann. The morning after our arrival we met Oblt. Assi Hahn, *Staffelkapitän* of the new 4. *Staffel*. Immediately he stated to Bolze and me, 'you will be in my *Staffel*'. At this time he was 25 years old, we were three years his junior.

"After a Spring spent in Nordholz, which brought many adventuresome flights over the north sea but very little contact with the enemy, the French campaign started in earnest on 10 May 1940. I almost always flew as Assi Hahn's *Katschmarek* (wingman) therefore witnessing most of his first 20 victories. After his 20th victory, Assi was awarded his Knight's Cross on 24 September 1940.

"He was a natural pilot and fighter leader. I was blessed with excellent eyesight, so while flying as his wingman I constantly searched the sky for enemy aircraft, alerting Assi to the danger as that was part of my job. At the end of the French campaign, we had to fly very, very often. Many times we flew four or five sorties a day. We flew the aircraft available because we could only fly for about 1 hour and 15 minutes then we would come back for another airplane. It was a hard time for us over the year 1940. Our adversary was the British Spitfire in air battles over England sometimes at the altitude of six or seven thousand meters.

"Assi mastered his airplane, playing in the sky and on the ground. He knew no inhibitions, no pussy footing! He was straight forward, direct. He scared many superiors more than his subordi-

nates whose weaknesses he readily forgave. He demanded as much from himself as he demanded from others. In that he could be so humane as one would not expect of him.

"Once during aerial combat over Normandy, several Spitfires chased the two of us. Assi tried to climb and get away, but increasingly lost speed. I watched with concern, the muzzle flashes directed at us from two Spitfires coming closer and closer from behind. At the very last moment Assi stood the machine on its head and dived down at full throttle. I needed all my strength to stay with him. We had finally shaken off our pursuers! After landing, he casually said to me, 'What do you think Meimberg? Didn't we show them the speed of a 109!!?' I was angry and countered *'Herr Oberleutnant*, we were hanging around there at too low a speed. Fifty kilometers more and we would have evaded them easily'. His response was disarming, surprising me and was unthinkable for a superior officer at that time and yet so typical for him as he exclaimed, 'How scared do you think I was?!?'

"During this time, Assi, Lt. Bolze and I would often patronize local drinking establishments in the evening. Our task was to make sure Assi did not get into any trouble as he frequently did. We would drink and eat, having a great time but guess who paid, Bolze and I!

"In those days spent with Assi, I got to know him, not only in the air, but during the hours on the ground, as one normally does not get to know another human being. We often worried about each other, he about me, me about him. I left Assi's 4. *Staffel*, as I had been promoted to *Staffelkapitän* of 3. *Staffel*, JG 2, 15 April 1941."

*Above; In front of "White 5"; Julius Meimberg, left, Assi Hahn center with his donkey
"Icko" and Siegfried Schnell on the right. Photo taken at Münster, Germany.*

Below; Assi in front of his "White 13", April 1940, Münster, Germany.

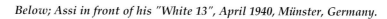

Lt. Julius Meimberg, 4. Staffel, wingman and life-long friend of Assi on "Icko"
in front of "White 3" April 1940, Münster, Germany.

On the occasion of Julius Meimberg's 65th birthday in 1982, Assi Hahn sent a letter of greetings and wishes "...to stay healthy so that we can see each other again." In this letter, Assi presents in greater detail the initial meeting of these two very close friends:

Frundsberg, 7 January 1982

"My dear Julius,

"In 1939, I established a *Jagdstaffel* in Zerbst that was equipped with the machine Me 109. Among the pilots that were to fly the Me 109 was a young *Leutnant* named Meimberg of Münster and a Catholic. Meimberg, I told him, you will first fly around the airfield. When you drive out the landing gear at 300 meters before you reach the landing cross, you only need to press and the machine will go down like an elevator to the landing cross. But leave off the gas. The only thing Meimberg remembered was the word elevator with which you can travel up and down. The last I remember was a 109 that approached the airfield edge at an altitude of 300 meters and went on the gas shortly before reaching the edge and climbed vertically toward the stratosphere. Since it had to tip down, crash, and explode any second, I did not want to lose any time and went to my office to write one of those painful letters to the dead pilot's mother in Münster. This letter was never finished because the dear departed reported back from his flight with a beaming face.

"The war had started, and what occurred now it was actually only the continuation of the Zerbst flight around the airfield. The *Staffel* was transferred to Haminkeln near Wesel on a meadow. The meadow was not particularly long but adequate for landing an Me 109.

"When we arrived above Haminkeln, I had the experienced *Feldwebel* Harbauer land first which he did well. The next one was Meimberg. It is an old custom of war that when somebody falls – in one instance for the fatherland, in another due to the fatherland or once for Wallenstein (military leaders in the Thirty Years War, 1618-1648) or for the Kaiser – in any case, somebody is killed in the war and his name is chiseled in stone, which would not have occurred had he not died. Meimberg decided not to fall for anybody but onto something and that was the cross. I was still airborne when this happened and grew mad that my first activity in Haminkeln would have to be letter writing to Mrs. Meimberg in Münster. When I landed as the last one, Meimberg reported completely healthy and beaming from the rollover.

"On 14 May, the *Staffel* was located at the Belgian troop exercise field Peer. It was warm and hazy when the *Staffel* started in the area south of Brussels when we had the first contact with the enemy. We were suddenly involved in a dogfight against a *Staffel* of Hurricanes close to the ground and even shot down our first enemies. In the general chaos we lost sight of each other, and when I returned to Peer, I worried who of us would not return. My *Katschmarek* Meimberg was no longer next to me, his first air battle just could not have been his last one. Finally, everybody had landed, only Meimberg was missing.

"I withdrew to my office and wrote to Mrs. Meimberg in Münster, that her son had fallen for the people, and the fatherland ---. We missed him terribly, his estate was in order. It was good that the letter was never mailed because it would have made a bad impression on the survivors, a part of the estate was buried later by Meimberg himself. To make a long story short, around noon of the next day he reported back in the best of health from the enemy flight and from Germany where he had strayed. I resolved not to write any more letters to Mrs. Meimberg from now on.

"And there would have been reason for it after all. A bit later an ear splitting noise disrupted the quietude of the *Staffel* airfield. Meimberg had dismantled the enemy ammunition which did not tolerate this well. Surely I could write a whole book about this, but from what I have written up to here makes it clear even to the least soul that this boy will not get old.

"Well, dear Julius, spend your great day with your large family and many friends and acquaintances as is common for folks like us.

Be embraced with cordial congratulations by

Gisela and Your Old Assi

An abandoned French Bloch 152.

A pilot from JG 2 checking out the Bloch 152.

A Bf 109 E "White 11" or "White 14" now with the "Richthofen" emblem "R" in a silver shield. Other than **Oberleutnant** *Hahn, second from the left, the names of these* **Luftwaffe** *officers are unknown. The* **Oberleutnant** *on the far left and the* **Oberleutnant** *right are both wearing WWI pilot's wings and WWI Iron Cross I class awards. Early Summer 1940.*

On 11 May 1940, Assi's wingman Lt. Julius Meimberg, suffered a severe crash landing that flipped his "White 1" over on its back. This happened at Hamminkeln, north of Wesel, Germany.

*A **Schwarm** of 7. Staffel Bf 109 Es flying over the Seine river in France, near La Havre on 23 August 1940. Note the White bands on the rear fuselage, an early application of that distinctive III. **Gruppe** marking. "White 4", "White 5" and "White 8" are visible; a "**Richthofen**" unit emblem can be seen on "White 5".*

During the summer of 1940, JG 2 was based at the elegant Chateau Beaumont-le-Roger, where Assi gathered his treasured menagerie of animals. Julius Meimberg tells, "Assi loved life, nature and animals. Here too, he broke through the usual constraints and collected ever more new animals until we had an actual little zoo in Beaumont-le-Roger. After the war, he enjoyed his superb cactus garden first in Germany and then later at his home in Southern France."

His animal collection included first and foremost, his beloved Harlequin black and white male Great Dane[5] dog "Lux" a constant companion to Assi and playmate to the other members of the unit. Lux would always greet the returning aircraft after a mission. Possessing the uncanny ability to find his master's machine, Lux would leap up on the fuselage side as Assi opened the canopy to dismount.

A bear cub named "Wumm" was given to Assi on behalf of the unit by the Berlin Zoo. Everyone found great sport in taking turns wrestling with this mischievous cub. As the bear grew, generally the men came out the looser, however, because of Assi's powerful build, he oftentimes overpowered the playful Wumm.

Another favorite was "Icko", the donkey. He had been with the men at earlier stations where they would occasionally ride him, especially when clowning around. The large Eagle-Owl, an *Uhu* named "Moritz" was kept in a large pen together with a parrot, pheasant, other miscellaneous birds, chickens and pigs.

Oblt. Assi Hahn was awarded the coveted Knight's Cross to the Iron Cross on 24 September 1940, one day after his 20th victory over a Spitfire shot down over Rochester England.

Leading the III. *Gruppe* of JG 2 since 24 September 1940 was Hptm. Otto Bertram one of three brothers serving in the *Luftwaffe*. His two brothers had recently been killed in combat, and according to *Luftwaffe* regulations, the surviving sibling would be ordered released from combat duty.

Therefore, on 28 October 1940, he was awarded the Knight's Cross and returned to Germany for further non-combat duty. After the departure of Hptm. Otto Bertram, the next day Assi Hahn was promoted to *Hauptmann* and elevated to *Gruppenkommandeur* of III./JG 2.

Now proudly wearing his Knight's Cross awarded on 24 September 1940, Assi stands in front of his Bf 109 E-4 "White 14". Note all Yellow cowling. (Aircraft No. 3)

*Oblt. Hahn sitting in his "White 14" Bf 109 E-4, 4./JG 2.
Note head armor in canopy, this "Richthofen" emblem has
a simple outline shield. He is holding his flight helmet
model LKpN101. This is the machine he was flying and
crash landed in the famous "The Bog Ghost" story.*

*Pointing at his 20th victory bar on the rudder of "White 14".
Assi scored this victory over a Spitfire on 23 September 1940.
Note the Light Blue panel behind the White victory bars out-
lined in Black and the Yellow top and bottom portions.*

*Carl-Hans Röders in his Bf 109 E. Note the
White shield and Red "R" emblem of JG 2
"Richthofen". Oblt. Röders was KIA as
Staffelkapitän of 9./JG 2 on 23 June 1941 flying
a Bf 109 F-2 W. Nr. 6764.*

Assi lecturing his wingman, Lt. Julius Meimberg in front of Assi's "White 14". "This was staged strictly for the camera", Meimberg commented when interviewed by the author in 1986. Note the long II. Gruppe bar. Photo taken late September 1940.

Lt. Meimberg sitting on his Bf 109 E with 5 victory bars on the Yellow rudder. 6 September 1940.

Fw. Siegfried Schnell flew in Assi's 4. Staffel. He is shown here pointing at the Yellow rudder with eleven victory bars on his Bf 109 E, W. Nr. 1232. Note Light Blue behind theWhite bars. Mid September 1940.

Obfw. Segfried Schnell next to Hahn. Note the 13 victory bars on the rudder of Schnell's aircraft, Bf 109 E. 30 September 1940

Awarded his Knight's Cross on 5 September 1940, here Lt. Werner Machold, a member of 9./JG 2 stands in front of his Bf 109 E.

Proud of their home-town boy, the city of Gotha closely followed Assi's achievements and held celebrations in his honor. Invitations were offered to speak at the academic high school, Assi's photos was hung in a place of honor, special hunting privileges were offered by the local forestry office, and the *Oberburgermeister* (Mayor) extended the great honor for Assi Hahn to sign the Golden Book of the City of Gotha.[6]

From a newspaper article by war correspondent Jochen Scheurmann, dated 1 November 1941, Assi Hahn relates the story of his only crash "...he experienced in the long years of his pilot career. Yes, he is mightily proud that he never crashed his machine. Therefore, he has the right to get very angry when one of his people does a crash landing, because he himself has never damaged his Me 109. Except for one single time. He now talks about the incident with a grin."

Hahn's Bf 109 E-4 after he was promoted to **Gruppenkommandeur** *of III./JG 2 on 29 October 1940. On 6 November he was credited with his 22nd victory recorded here on the Yellow rudder. The all-Yellow cowl can be seen along with the White shield of the* **"Richthofen"** *emblem. (Aircraft No. 4)*

*"Yellow 2" Bf 109 E-4 of Oblt. Helmut Wick **Staffelkapitän** of 3./JG 2, with 18 victory bars on the rudder. The last victory was a Hurricane on 16 August 1940. This is the same aircraft he later flew as **Gruppenkommandeur** of I./JG 2, after 10 October 1940. Note the Blue pennant emblem on the engine cowling and Wick's personal bird emblem just in front of the Yellow 2. The typical sponge-applied, stippled camouflage is clearly evident.*

Detail of rare, unusual personal bird emblem of Helmut Wick which is located just in front of the Yellow "2" as seen in enlarged area (right) of top photo.

Above: Helmut Wick, center, has just been promoted to **Hauptmann.** *While the new "pip" is being sewed on his left shoulder strap, Assi Hahn, left, holds the one for the right shoulder strap.*

Left: Helmut Wick was awarded Oak Leaves to his Knight's Cross on 6 October 1940, then promoted to **Major** *on 17 October and advanced to* **Geschwaderkommodore** *of JG 2 on 20 that same month. His meteoric career ended when he was killed on 28 November 1940.*

Above; A White shield with Red "R" emblem.

Left; A technician painting on the "Richthofen" emblem on a Bf 109. Note the White shield.

Chapter 2 Notes:

1. Initially two Hurricanes were claimed on this day, but only one was officially credited to Assi. Hans Ring.
2. Hahn was promoted to *Hauptman* 29 October 1940.
3. Julius Meimberg would later be assigned to *Staffelkapitän* of 3./JG 2, then 11./JG 2. On 20 April 1944 he became *Kommandeur* of II./JG 53, ultimately flying over 250 missions always against Western opponents.
4. From a speech given at Assi Hahn's funeral service in December 1982 and a published letter written to *Jägerblatt*, the magazine of the *Gemeinshaft der Jagdflieger*. Letter fur-

nished to the author from Julius Meimberg. Notes from personal interview and correspondence of Julius Meimberg by the author, 1998, 2001, 2002.
5. The author also had the privilege of owning one of these magnificent Harlequin Great Danes for ten years. Known for their devotion and gentleness, Assi's love for his Lux is readily understandable.
6. Original documents and telegrams from the city of Gotha in author's collection.

Chapter Three
The Bog Ghost

Regarding Assi Hahn's singular crash, Julius Meimberg also recalls, "The most dramatic event was when we lost orientation in transit because of a storm front northeast of Mont St. Michel. Our fuel supply forced us to land soon. Assi lowered his landing gear for a landing on a harmless looking meadow. I saw to my horror he was setting down in a bog.

"I had no radio contact with him and flew to his side to warn him, but he was looking down so I watched helplessly while his plane rolled over.

"But then, what a miracle, the front part emerged from the bog, the airplane had broken apart. The motor block and cockpit stuck out of the moor, the canopy hood was opened and Assi waved at me. Unbelievable!

"His walk home to the unit as the 'bog ghost' supplied all *Geschwadern* with abundant conversation material."

The following story was possibly written by Assi, in the third person, about this incident:

The Bog Ghost

After six months of uninterrupted attacks on London, the German *Luftwaffe* discontinued the "Battle of Britain" without having reached its stated goal, namely to affect a capitulation. September 1940 came to an end, and the units of the two German *Luftflotten* had lost great numbers of flying personnel. They were transferred from the Channel Coast to the French hinterland or to their homes to heal the sustained wounds and to prepare for new missions.

Of the German *Jagdgeschwadern* involved in the London offensive, one did not get to rest, the *Jagdgeschwader "Richthofen"*. The battle tested *Staffel* with the red "R" on their machines left their previous staging areas around Calais-Dunkerque but only to resume the battle at a different place under far more difficult geographical conditions.

The young leader with the grand tradition had moved to the top of the most successful German fighter pilots a with unique series of aerial victories and had succeeded in gaining permission that his men could continue to attack the British coast from Normandy and Brittany. The valiant pilots flew these missions from Cherbourg and Le Havre to the British coast at a distance of 180 km with the wind-swept waves of the Channel below them and in most cases the lurking Spitfires above them at previously unknown altitudes of 10 to 1100 meters.

There was only time for a 10 to 15 minute aerial battle over the British continent, after which they had to turn back to fly the 180 km to the French coast with the last liters of fuel. Woe to the machine that got engine damage or an unfortunate hit in the radiator during the mission - it would not reach the continent, and many comrades were lost at the sea during those weeks.

Suddenly and completely unexpectedly in the middle of these missions, the *Geschwader* was ordered in late October to transfer without delay to an airfield close to Biarritz.

The *Staffelkapitän* of 4. *Staffel* discusses the flight route with his pilots. He will lead the first *Schwarm*, *Leutnant* Meimberg the second and *Feldwebel* Sigfried Schnell the third. Then comes the start. The *Staffel* flies above the wide plains of Normandy and soon over the Loire valley and low over this garden of France with its magnificent castles and parks to reach Tours shortly before darkness falls. The 4. *Staffel* continues flying on the next morning over the French western provinces southward. Lt. Meimberg recognizes on the map the familiar name Cognac, there are vineyards as far as the eye can see. The mouth of river they approach is the Gironde and the large city, more inland is Bordeaux. The Messerschmitts land next to the gigantic Fw 200 Condors.

Two or three Messerschmitts would fit comfortably under the big brother's wing, and finally the small elegant fighters are assembled like chicks around the hen. The crews of these opposites of the *Luftwaffe*, the giants and the dwarfs, shake hands.

Just prior to the arrival of the Messerschmitts, a Short Sunderland, the first flying fortress, a very slow but heavily armed British flying boat, landed suddenly on the Gironde next to a German customs boat, took the surprised 8 man crew prisoner and moved them on board, subsequently sank the customs boat with the board canon and then started unmolested and somewhat heavier than before. North of Bordeaux over a German training airfield, the British flying boat wiggled its wings. It forced two German *Jagdschule* planes to land with strong defense fire; they had started immediately to shoot the "fat flounder" down. Then the Sunderland vanished at low altitude in the direction of the sea with its captives.

The new arrivals had missed this event. The Channel hunters became attentive because nobody would have expected the British this far south, and the fighter pilots had expected this excursion to the Biskaya to be a vacation from the hard work in the north.

It turns out to be a vacation after all. The reason for the transfer to the Pyrenees is revealed to the *Staffelkapitän* a few hours later in Biarritz: In the next few days, a meeting of the three heads of state of Spain, France and Italy will take place at the French border train station Hendaye. The *"Richthofen"* fighters were ordered here for their protection.

And so, a *Rotte*, (two machines), is flying from dawn to dusk for protection over the special train. It is a real joy to fly above the white foam of the Biskaya, over palms, the hotel palaces of Biarritz to St. Sebastian and along the rocky cliffs of the Pyrenees - "*Jagdflieger*, you are a lucky lad," is an old, garbled hunter's idiom. This "dolce far niente" (sweet idleness) lasts only a few days, then the fighters at the Channel coast call their comrades back because reinforcements are urgently needed up there.

Hptm. Hahn leads the *Staffel* to Bordeaux. Here, the weather office forbids the continued flight to the north. It is also raining in Bordeaux, but flying is possible. It is incomprehensible what the weather frogs are saying. There is supposedly a storm front moving from England over north western France, the clouds are not even 100 meters high on the stretch to Tours, and vision is reduced to 200 meters in rain and snow showers.

The *Staffelkapitän* decides grimly to remain in Bordeaux. But when the weather situation does not change, he selects another course. Why fly via Tours to Le Havre when the inland weather is so bad, we'll try the east. In Brest is a forward command post of the *Geschwader*. Hptm. Hahn decides to fly along the coast despite the objection of the weather office. The Breton war harbor is reached without major difficulties. It is raining hard throughout the whole journey but who cares? At the target harbor, the weather is significantly better, the sun even tries to peak through the clouds.

The 4. *Staffel* is urgently needed, but not in Brest, rather in Le Havre. Damn, the same weather news as in Bordeaux, again this storm and rain front from England! Indeed, the command post in Brest has had no flight connection with the *Geschwader* south of Le Havre, since the day before yesterday. The *Staffel* must stay in Brest overnight. This is annoying. The next morning, there is bright sunshine over Brittany. But at the moment when the *Staffel* is getting ready to start, a Ju 52 is returning to the airfield. It wanted to get to Paris but had to turn back because it was completely iced up north of Rennes due to a bad weather front. From Le Havre, one yell for help after the other is received. The British are taking advantage of the absence of the II. *Gruppe* and of the bad weather by increasing their bomber missions. Le Havre needs the 4. *Staffel* urgently!

At noon, the sky over Brest is cloudless, but the weather report remains the same. Then Hptm. Hahn decides to investigate by himself if he can make it to Le Havre. He takes his two experienced *Schwarmführer* Lt. Meimberg and Fw. Schnell along. The three start on 11 November[1] at 17:05 hours from Brest to Le Havre.

The *Kapitän* had arranged before his start that Le Havre would call immediately if the stretch could be flown and that the rest of *Staffel* should then follow. If the flight could not be concluded against all probability, they would either return to Brest or make a landing at one of the airfields of Brittany or Normandy.

The three Me 109s are flying eastward along the Brittany coast.[2] They are at an altitude of about 1000 meters, Meimberg is flying on the left and Schnell on the right of the boss. There are clouds in the far south, they do not matter. On their right, they see Morlaix, then St. Brieuc. Soon Dinard with the old Corsair city St. Malo is below the *"Richthofen" Kette*, (three aircraft) Mont St. Michel looks like a Gothic pyramid rising from the ocean. None of the three flyers notice the suddenly darkening horizon. They are gazing down at this wonder of world sinking in the golden evening light into the ocean. Further north, two aircraft contrails sneak between the channel islands and then continue toward Cherbourg.

While they are awed by this singularly beautiful sight, a cloud layer coming from the east moves over the aircraft, it sinks rapidly, and near Avranches the clouds reach only 300 meters. The sun has long faded in the west, suddenly is gets very dark, snow-rain is falling on the cabin and there is no visibility.

Why is Assi not turning back the other two pilots wonder, but they hear the familiar voice in the radio: "Bad weather formation!" They immediately go into this flight formation and light the board illumination. Now all three, one after the other, roar at the lowest possible altitude over the pitch black landscape. It is impossible to keep the orientation in this situation. Certainly, Assi had a plan when he did not turn back after the bad weather front reached them, but he decided to cross the peninsula Contentin.

At the moment, when "bad weather formation" is ordered, the leader of the unit is flying in front, and the following pilot only sees the red rear lights of the one in front of him and has nothing else to do but to follow closely. Hptm. Hahn is aware of that. He has the responsibility for his splendid comrades; he does not fly for himself, he is flying for three, and his comrades are hanging on him trusting him blindly. He considers: It is too late to return to Brest, there is not enough fuel. He also rejects the thought of turning back in this wild weather to reach one of the airfields in Brittany.

In that instance, they would have to traverse the whole distance with bad weather again. But when continuing toward the northeast, it could only be a few minutes before they cross the peninsula at whose northern coast Cherbourg is located, and then they would reach the Channel coast of Normandy. After that, following the coast via Caen to Beauville should be easy, and the jump over the mouth of the Seine to Le Havre does not even need to be mentioned.

So the three Me 109s roar tightly aligned toward the northeast over the inlets and willows between Avranches and the mouth of the Vire in wild jumps over the hedges. They suddenly notice the limitations of human vision. One should be able to see more, the eyes are too small. Hopefully there is no church steeple, no chimney or some other high obstacle along the way, this would be fatal because they can only see vertically down and there is only a milky soup in the front. Where is the end of this damned stretch of land, Assi is wondering.

Sweat drips from his forehead and each muscle is tensed. Again and again he tries to penetrate this dangerous darkness before him with his eyes, but in vain, no horizon can be seen. Then, suddenly, the terra firma ends and the almost back darkness cedes to a monotonous leaden gray, the ocean is reached, sky and earth flow together. Nobody can say where the sea starts and ends, the three flyers are surrounded on all sides by a dense dark fog. They cannot discern a stretch of beach where they could fly along. The situation is far more dangerous than over the threatening black ground, it is almost hopeless!

He must act fast now, if a rescue is even possible. How high are we above the sea level, the *Hauptmann* is wondering; the altimeter shows zero. He tries desperately not to move the control stick so that he is not giving up a meter of altitude.

Behind him, there are the position lights of the comrades trusting in God and in him, the *Staffelkapitän*; he has no time to think. There is only one possibility, flying a return curve. The course must be changed by 180° to reach land again. He dares an attempt even though it does not promise much a success. It can only be done in the wobbly and unstable Messerschmitt without any horizon and close to the ground when a guardian angle is sitting on the wing, and he is indeed.

Assi in the lead machine lowers the left wing. Fractions of seconds will decide if it gets into the water, but nothing happens. The three pilots pull their birds around, and finally, almost gingerly, the lead machine is straight again. If there were time, one would take a deep breath. But there is no time. The heart thumps on, it is still unclear if the plane will fall into the sea during the next moment or if it will ascent vertically, lose speed and crash down. Finally, Assi's voice is heard in the microphone: "We made it!" The coast was reached.

As if the danger was dispelled with the feeling of terra firma below, Assi decides to make an emergency landing on the next larger meadow - what else could be done? It is now too late to reach the next airfield in Brittany, and the Messerschmitts roar above a wide meadow overgrown with heather appearing suddenly below them. This lifeline is sent by God, here we will land. Again his voice in the microphone: "We'll land. I go down first, and only after I have taxied to a stop, the next will follow!" The radio is switched off. Prior to an emergency landing, the whole electrical circuit in the airplane is switched off so that a possible spark creating a fire is prevented in the event of a crash.

Assi Hahn starts his landing procedure in a somewhat tight curve. The landing gear descends and the landing flaps are turned out, then the Me 109 glides down. Lt. Meimberg who is flying behind Assi screams into the microphone - in vain, because the he cannot hear it any longer. Meimberg had recognized from the first moment that the large brown meadow is not heather but a treacherous bog; after all, he had been in the labor service in the Emsland (northwestern German region around the mouth of the river Ems, known for its marshy bog lands). But he cannot avert the unavoidable. He flies desperately past Assi while waving and wiggling, but the terrible event occurs.

The machine below him sets down at almost 200 km/h. The landing gear slams into the bog, disengages and after an incredibly fast summersault the plane crashes with its back into the bog and breaks into two pieces behind the cabin. The front half with motor and cabin is catapulted by a giant's fist back into the air, about 20 meters high, turns a summersault, hits the bog for a second time at a distance of about 50 meters from the tail end that is standing upright in the bog. Meimberg cannot see any more, he loses the crash site and is busy with himself. He cannot help anyway, the Assi down there will not need any help; what a tragedy that it had to end this way!

However, this is my no means the "end" for Hptm. Assi Hahn. After the noise from the last bursting crash is over and all is quiet, he notices to his surprise that he is still alive. A first muscle play in the face and a careful movement of his arms and legs convince him of the correctness of his assumption. He notices with wonder that everything is intact. His arms and legs obey him; there is only an insignificant impact wound at his forehead.

How lucky that he was especially tightly strapped in today. As if the ground engineer in Brest had anticipated trouble when he pulled the straps so tightly as if a dangerous criminal was to be shackled; the safety belts undoubtedly saved his life.

The wind blows into the cabin behind the seat. Everything that used to be there is gone. He opens the safety belts with one grasp and the parachute with another. The cabin opens without trouble because the machine, thank God, is not lying on its back. In seconds Assi is standing on the wing. "Summersault King at Hell's Speed" are his first words. That used to be an American action movie he had enormously admired in his youth. Now he was a "Salto King" of the kind that had never been shown in any movie.

He looks around while standing on the wing next to the cabin. There is only the rain and storm whipped dusk, and wild cloud fragments fly as low as houses. As much as his eyes try, nowhere can he find a place of rescue; he is searching in vain. Once in a while the endless showers stop, and the horizon becomes clearer; in such a moment he can see a forest far to the north; there he can maybe find rescue.

Assi's deliberations are clear, he cannot spend the night here on the moor and he must leave this devil's area as quickly as possible before it is completely dark! At a place with a forest, there would be no moor; and the forest was in the north, so he must start the march toward the north immediately and without wasting any time.

But it will be very exhausting in the heavy pilot's outfit as he is wearing the heavy leather trousers in warm fur boots, two flares with a flare gun are tied below his knees, and a light "channel blouse" all protected from cold by a thick fur jacket with a high collar. He exchanges the pilot's cap against a visor cap and pinches the new yellow briefcase under his arm, slings the Leica camera over his shoulder and begins his march that is intended to bring him to safety but almost ends in disaster.

With the very first step from the firm wing to the harmless looking ground, his legs sink into a glutinous, sucking ooze, he sinks fast, within 10 seconds he is standing in the mud up to his knees. When he pulls the legs up, the wide fur boots remain in the muck - thank God, they are gone, walking in them would have been impossible anyway. It becomes clear that the path out of the bog will be devilish jumping process; standing is impossible, and even when hurrying, it cannot be prevented that the foot sinks in far above the ankle.

The constant freeing one foot from the sucking moor clutches and offering the other foot to the vicious mud in the next moment takes much strength. Assi is in the same situation as bears when they learn to dance. Bears are placed on hot sheet metal where they cannot stand because their paws would burn, and so they lift their feet alternatively and begin to dance. In this case, there is no dancing but the effect of the bog below the feet is the same as the hot sheet metal, he cannot stop and stand, he must lift his feet, must walk, always walk; even the shortest respite

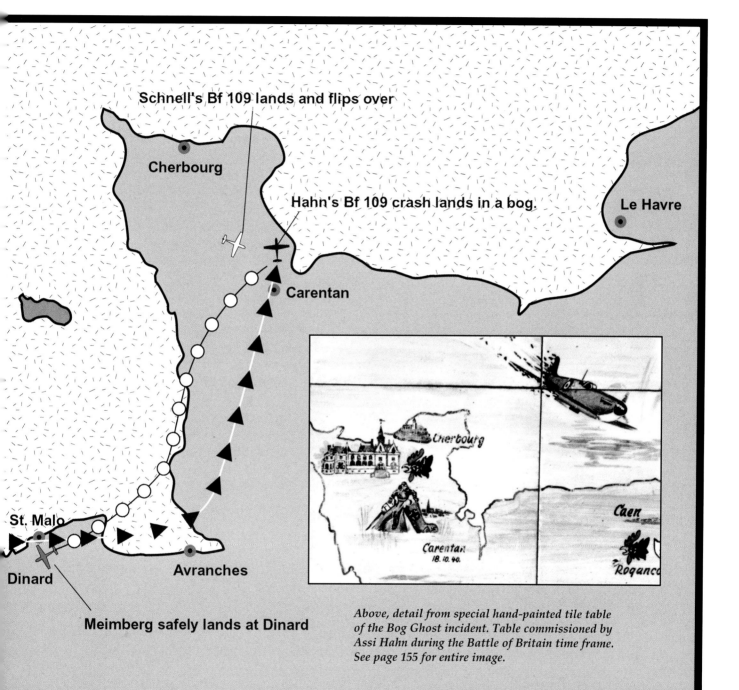

Schnell's Bf 109 lands and flips over

Cherbourg

Hahn's Bf 109 crash lands in a bog.

Le Havre

Carentan

St. Malo

Dinard

Avranches

Meimberg safely lands at Dinard

Above, detail from special hand-painted tile table of the Bog Ghost incident. Table commissioned by Assi Hahn during the Battle of Britain time frame. See page 155 for entire image.

would bring death, only walking can lead to salvation. Therefore, Assi walks haphazardly in the direction where he believes to have seen the forest earlier. How unlucky that he is not wearing his wrist compass today; he can only rely on his instincts; hopefully he is not wrong.

It was 1800 hours when he started the march. Now half an hour has passed, and there is no end in sight, but it is getting darker, the storm is raging, there is whistling and whispering over the moor. The delayed effects of the hundred per cent crash landing are gradually noticeable. The matter did not proceed without a slight concussion; he is freezing and then feels feverish as a reaction to the crash, but this does not matter; at this moment, escaping the bog as quickly as possible is paramount. But this goal seems to be far away at this time.

After walking for an hour, his progress is impeded by a ditch that is about 10 meters wide. Because there is no chance to get across, Assi changes direction and walks along the ditch hoping to find a bridge or a boat somewhere, but nothing of the sort is visible.

In the meantime, night has fallen. It is impossible to make out any compass direction, the low clouds whirl ghostlike above the moving, living bog. He has forgotten where he saw the forest. The only guideline has been the ditch for almost an hour now. Suddenly, there is a high silhouette on his left. Maybe a tree; a wonderful thought, there he could rest and would not have to continue fighting in the viscous bog. Possibly he could stand still, maybe even sit down. The tree is only a stone's throw away, Assi runs toward it, and then he is confronted with the tail of his Messerschmitt standing upright in a bog. A terrible disappointment!

For two hours he has been running futile around the bog, for two hours he had to pull his legs from the sucking fetters, and now he is at the same point where he had started this hike. A state of apathy follows the previous tension of body and spirit. He suddenly feels tired and desires nothing more than to lie down and to sleep. Assi drags himself painfully for another 50 meters to the location of the other part of his airplane. He wants to sit in the cabin and spend the night there. By morning, the weather will surely have improved and it should not be a problem to get out of the bog in daylight and after a good rest.

But when he arrives, he realizes that the crashed plane has shifted. The heavy motor is completely submerged and pulled the wing and the cabin that is half filled with water deeper into the bog. It is clear to see that the machine will have completely vanished within a few hours. What a horrible thought! Had there only been a slight flip during the crash landing, it would have been impossible to escape from the cabin and slowly, with the head down, he would have been submerged in the moor water within a few hours. As it happened he was saved from being found in a few thousand years as a well preserved bog body to be exhibited in a prehistoric museum; this should be reason enough in the current situation not to capitulate but to fight for freedom. No, this can never be the end!

Assi takes the pistol and fires off a flare. A green double star explodes at the rim of the clouds. Pale deathlike light spreads over the bog for short moments, then everything is black and dark as before. Placing his hands around his mouth, he calls "Halloooo, hallooo, haaaloo, heeeelp, heeeelp!" The sound diminishes in the distance, the storm carries it away, pulls the words apart, but no answer, echo, resonance comes from anywhere! But isn't there a call, far away, dim? He holds his breath and listens, he is not deceived, somewhere in a distance a dog is barking. This bark comes from the opposite direction of his previous march, but the dog can replace the compass, he can bring salvation.

He still has 15 flares. If he fires 1 flare at intervals of 20 minutes and yells loudly, the dog will surely bark again, and where there is a dog, there are also people and there will be no more bog. He resolves to walk in that direction, as long as he can keep the course. When this is no longer possible, he will send up another flare and the dog will bark again. This must be the way out.

He starts walking without hesitation, and he feels as if he had a rest, refreshed and strengthened with new hope. When he shoots the second flare after a while, the dog barks clearly in his marching direction, far away. The distance is hard to guess, but it must be at least several kilometers.

Again he is calling through the night that becomes a bit calmer. Haaaalloo, heeelp! But there is no answer. In the meantime, the sky over the bog becomes red, green and white four times, and more than an hour must have passed since the second start from the crash site. Then, a wide black ditch stops him. Another shot from the flare gun reveals that he must follow the path from the other side of the water. The dog's bark is clearly audible, and it seems as if people responded to his cries for help, but his ears are ringing and he cannot be certain. To avoid walking at the side of the ditch in a circle as before in search of a boat or a vehicle, Assi decides to swim to the other side. But the clothes must get over there in a dry state.

The leather trousers, shirt, underpants are knotted into a package and catapulted forcefully to the other side. That's where they were to land, but a watery response reveals that the throw was too short and they landed in the water. With that, the listed pieces of clothing are also lost and his continued march will have to proceed with a substantially lighter load. The cap suffers the same fate as the clothing package; it also falls into the water somewhere. He carefully packs the last remaining piece of clothing, the fur jacket into the briefcase together with the Leica, and throws it across from its handle like a sling ball.

Carrying the pistol with the flares and the *Ritterkreuz* in his right fist, Assi crosses through the warm brackish water with a few swimming motions, collects the briefcase and the fur vest in the light of another flare and continues the march in the direction of the dog.

The flares are almost used up; he can only shoot three more times, that is the end, then the moor must be behind him. He lengthens the intervals to half an hour as it is impossible to keep on course for longer than that. But what happens when the last flare is gone and land has not been reached and the dog does not bark? Gradually, fatigue takes over, his strength is ebbing. After the flare, the dog's bark is very faint. Does this dog exist? Is the bark only an acoustic will o' whisp that he pursued for hours on end only to return to the point of departure?

The rain has slowed. Bits of clouds pass overhead. Many bog stories he had heard or read with terror as a child come forth in his memory. In the midst of these thoughts, a wide dark band is appearing in front of him, and the *Hauptmann* is standing for the third time in front of this fiendish dead river.

Now the last doubt is dispelled if the dog ever barked; all this was delusion, he only waked around the bog in circles. The last flare is inserted in the gun. When it explodes red near the clouds, his nerves are taut - will the dog bark? - He does not! Neither on the other side of the ditch, nor anywhere else is there an answer to his calls, his desperate yells.

Nonetheless, Assi has the feeling that he went on the right course; how easy it would be if there were stars. But a glance up to the sky is disappointing. He does not know why, but an inner voice urges him to cross the ditch once more, and with a fast decision he throws the briefcase across and he jumps again in the strangely warm heavy water. From the other side, he continues his march in the previous direction.

Around midnight, the rain finally stops, and the sky is getting lighter, and the ground, covered now with high cattails, rapidly turns firmer. Suddenly, a high black thing is in front of him, the ground is firm and in the next moment he embraces an old cracked tree like a lover, he wants to kiss the craggy bark. His knees buckle and he is sinking down, exhausted. But he jumps up again; the lack of pants proved disadvantageous, and so he rests upright, leaning at the old trunk - his first pause.

But soon it gets noticeably cold and he starts again to keep from freezing. He penetrates several thorny hedges, gets scratched in the thorns, tears through spikes, crosses meadows, climbs over stone fences and finally reaches a sunken road after sliding down a steep incline. This is a first chance to get to people. His repeated calls were unanswered until now, and Assi has the nagging feeling that people are fleeing from him. In the meantime, the moon comes through the clouds, its pale light falls into the gorge, makes long shadows, vanishes and returns. The whole situation appears ghostlike.

Not far from a sharp curve in the road, the clatter of hooves is audible; it comes closer fast. Assi steps into the moon shade, and soon a rider on a heavy Norman field horse approaches slowly around the curve. When he is at a distance of about 20 meters, Assi jumps in front of the rider: "Monsieur, je suis un officier Allemande" (Sir, I am a German officer), but he does not get any further. As if he has just seen the devil, the rider turns on the hind legs and dashes, as if chased by all furies, back into the sunken road. Now it is quite clear that people are fleeing from him for some reason, in any case to avoid a meeting with a crashed pilot. He walks even faster because he needs people. He is unbearably thirsty. His naked feet not used to marching are hurting badly. It is quite cold.

Finally, after about half an hour, a living fence and then a large wooden gate appear in front of him. It is one of the farms in Normandy. It is locked securely, but he can see the house behind the fence, and a shy light comes from the closed shutters.

When nobody reacts to his prolonged knocking, Assi throws the briefcase across the gate and climbs after it despite the warning sign "Chien mechant" (Beware of Dog). When he arrives in the courtyard, no dog attacks him, the house door is locked, but he can hear voices that fade into the background. Clearly people are fleeing from him here too, and Assi, with his last strength, throws himself into the door that crashes out of its lock.

A Norman kitchen is in front of him; a woman is trying to lift a child out of a cradle, but when the door crashes open and she sees the late guest, she screams briefly and sinks to the ground next to the cradle with the child in her arms. In that moment, two old Normans appear from a different door, one is carrying a long, ground axe and the other holds an equally fearsome cudgel.

"Je suis un officier Allemande," Assi speaks in French and tries to explain to the two who approach him threateningly as if they could not hear him. He cannot evade them much further and is already pushed into a corner of the room. Suddenly a devil stares from the wall at him, a black hellish face with piercing white eyes and mud caked hair over a high fur collar, dried blood mixed with mud is glued to the left side of his face. Shocked, he wants to move away from this creature, but then he recognizes the mirror. Quickly he fills his hand with water from a buck-

et and washes the gluey bog mud from his face. When the first bit of white skin is visible, his two adversaries stop their pursuit. Assi quickly puts his whole head into the bucket and washes off the sticky mud and begins to tell his story once more, namely that he is a German officer whose machine crashed in the bog and that he has been running in the bog for more than six hours by now.

The Normans do not listen, and while one takes care of the woman prone on the floor, the other vanishes through a back door and returns with a type of woolen underpants which he offers to the stranger with unintelligible words. After his lower body is encased in these pants, his self-confidence significantly increases. A glass of milk slackens the burning thirst, and soon the recovered farmer's wife brings a large bowl with steaming potatoes mixed with ham. These are no small amounts that Assi gobbles with true hunger, they taste marvelous and cider is drunken with it. After a short time the guest feels so well in the warm kitchen as if the past six hours had never happened. Unfortunately, all attempts at communication are fruitless. The hosts do not understand their guest and vice versa.

When Assi asks repeatedly about the Commandanture Allemande (German Command Post), one of the men brings a pair of thick socks and Dutch wooden clogs, and after a cordial good-bye from the two others, the new friends climb on a heavy farm horse that was gotten out of a stable in a bad mood due to the unusual hour. While the old Norman is in front, Assi in his unique riding costume holds on to his front man - wooden clogs, his torso in a fur vest and with the yellow briefcase under his arm. They are riding onto the street like father and son in Goethe's *"Erlkönig"* (famous ballad by Germany's greatest poet about a father's attempt to save his son who, however, succumbs during the wild ride). They may have ridden for a kilometer when they see a house on the left; they stop at the garden gate and stiffly descend from the horse.

The Norman rings a hanging bell and after some time a man in a long house coat with a light in his hand appears. Assi again begins introducing himself again and to report his adventures since the previous afternoon. The stranger responds to his more or less correct French stutter, "you can speak German, I understand this language very well, I studied in Tübingen and am the priest of Qillebec."

The priest talks briefly to the farmer, shakes his hand and says good-bye; Assi also thanks his previous helper. Then the priest and the fighter pilot step into the cozy parish house. The priest does not seem to have slept yet; two empty Calvados bottles are shyly visible under a table next to an old wing chair, and on the table, self-confident and secure is a freshly opened bottle with Armagnac. While he cozily smokes his long pipe, the priest encourages his late guest to tell him his story - but only, after they assured each other of their greatest esteem several times with the noble brandy.

The German pilot starts his narrative with his emergency landing and tells his French host of his miserable march through the bog in great detail. The listener's eyes grow bigger, and after a short time he interrupts the report and starts talking himself:

"*Herr Hauptmann*, my ministerial activities here at the border of Brittany are difficult. Old pagan customs and manifold superstitions are still living among these people as they did a 1000 years ago. In this area around the large moor lives an old legend of a bog ghost. It is said that the ghost comes up from the moor every hundred years and approaches the villages around the edge of the bog with lightning and terrible groans to steal the village children to take them into the bog.

"When we had such an unusually dark weather during the last two days even during the daylight, some old women started the rumor that the weather was the sure sign that the bog ghost was in the offing. People became restless because a weather of this nature was unknown for as long as anybody could remember. At the time when it turned really wild, some farmers saw a large bright bird shoot across the moor and then there was an unknown crashing sound in the bog. People listened and looked fearfully.

"Then everything was quiet for a long time, but toward nightfall the frightened people heard long howls and the whole sky was lit up in pale green, and twenty minutes later, there was a fiery red lightning over the bog and then again green after a quarter of an hour.

"Now the people came to me and asked me to research in the church books and in the chronicles when the bog ghost had last appeared. To calm them down, I searched through the old folios and found that the ghost was mentioned last in 1842. That was too much for the superstitious people, and my remark that only 98 years have passed and that it is unlikely that the ghost would make a mistake by 2 years fell to deaf ears.

"The men congregated with all manner of weaponry at the edge of the bog, while women and children fled to the south. I also went to the bog and saw that in certain intervals strange lengthy lightning flashes appeared over the moor and then when we clearly heard a voice in the lightning at 2000 hours, I could not hold my farmers back any longer and they have been fleeing on the street leading to the south."

Assi Hahn toasts the priest: "Well, you see, now the bog ghost is sitting incarnate in front of you. The colorful lightning flashes were my flares and I yelled for help only; but that even the last courageous people fled and surely took the dog with them almost sealed my fate."

"Too bad that the farmer left," the priest interrupts, "we must send somebody after the refugees immediately and make them turn back. The farmer who brought you here neither attends the church nor is he influenced by old superstitions; that's why he probably stayed."

A little later, the French priest and the German pilot are seen arm in arm on a cart traveling to Carentan, the next German post. They have drunken brotherhood (ceremonial toast after which they address each other no longer with the formal but with the familiar address) and repeat it on the cart several times. At the German watch, the *Feldwebel* on duty believes that the slightly tipsy "tramp" is crazy when he claims that he is *Hauptmann* Assi Hahn of the *Jagdgeschwader* "*Richthofen*".

It takes a while to convince the *Feldwebel* of the correctness of his statement. When Assi asks about Fw. Schnell or Lt. Meimberg, he is informed that Schnell is staying in the local Hotel de la Ville. After a few minutes Schnell is standing in front of his *Staffelkapitän*. It is hard to say who of the two has the more surprised face. Schnell is staring at his boss whom he watched flying over the bog and falling apart 10 hours ago. He had no doubt that he was gone but now he is standing alive in front of him in a rather cheerful mood.

After Schnell had seen the end of his *Staffelkapitän*, he was terribly upset and made an emergency landing on the next meadow which was too short and the ground was too soft. The airplane did not tolerate his strong braking and turned over. This could have been managed if the plane had not started to burn immediately. It was impossible to extricate himself from the fire, and it took some time before the first two farmers arrived at the crash site. The two Frenchmen saved his life, and a physician joined him soon and placed bandages on his face and hands. This is why he is how now white as a snowman, at least in his face. Schnell did not know what happened to Meimberg.

In the early morning hours, the two German fighter pilots together with the priest Bonifatius and the *Feldwebel* of the German Army guard celebrate "birthday" until sunrise. After a cordial good-bye from the minister who had become a friend, the two *Staffel* comrades leave

Carentan in a truck and reach the *Geschwader* airfield in Normandy. Here the black men of the ground personnel think that they are indeed seeing ghosts, when the two Aces of the *Staffel* who had been reported killed are suddenly standing in such strange attires in front of them.

Meimberg had kept his cool as the only one and had landed with the last drop in the tank on the airfield Dinard in the Bretagne. There he had reported to the *Geschwader* the certain death of his *Staffelkapitän* and the probable death of Fw. Schnell. Two journalists are present at the airfield and want to report the horrific story of the bog ghost immediately, but Assi gets into the Fieseler "Storch" and flies to the bog to find out if any parts of the machine such as weapons, radio or parachute could be salvaged from the crash site.

North of Carentan, the large bog is lying peacefully in bright sunshine. The bog is surrounded by two concentric ditches and looks like a shooting target from above. No remnant of his faithful Messerschmitt can be discovered. Everything looks like a brown meadow overgrown with heather."

 Fieseler Storch used by the III./JG 2 Stab coded 5E + KJ. Note White J 3 on the rudder.

Chapter 3 Notes:

1. This date 11 November 1940 is incorrect. The actual date is 18 October 1940. On 29 October, Assi was promoted to Hptm. and given the command of III. *Gruppe* leaving the 4. *Staffel*. In addition Siegfried Schnell is referred to as *Feldwebel* but he was promoted to *Leutnant* on 1 November 1940.

2. Assi was flying "White 14" Bf 109 E, (see photo). This is mentioned in the JG 2 publication "*Richthofen Jagdgruppe ein jahr im krieg, 1941.*" The story is related in this publication and refers to Assi as *Oberleutnant*, by 11 November he was a *Hauptmann*.

 This camera icon indicates image still from movie.

Chapter Four
The Messerschmitt Bf 109 F

Early in 1941 a new aircraft was introduced to III./JG 2, it was a sleek new version of the Bf 109, the F or *Frederich* series. Throughout the spring as deliveries would allow, more and more of these streamlined machines were integrated into service. Assi Hahn's first known Bf 109 F was an F-2 subtype, *Werknummer* 5749.[1] The III. *Gruppe* was now stationed at the French Chateau de Saint-Pol/Brias.

*Right; Gefechtsstand (head quarters) for III./JG 2 located at the Chateau de Saint Pol, France. Note III. **Gruppe** Hahn rooster emblem above and the **Staffeln** emblems on the roof's edge. From the left, 9. **Staffel**, 8. **Staffel** and 7. **Staffel**, summer 1941.*

Assi's sleek sports coupe with right-hand drive and a command pennant on the fender.

Hptm. Wilhelm Balthasar Kommodore *of JG 2 "Richthofen" served in the Condor Legion during the Spanish Civil War and was promoted to Geschwaderkommodore of JG 2 on 17 February 1941. Photo taken before he was awarded the Oak Leaves to the Knight's Cross on 2 July 1941. He was killed the next day, 3 July when a wing came off his Bf 109 F-4 and he crashed to his death.*

A pensive *Oblt. Hahn in the* Gefechtsstand *at St. Pol France, note the JG 2 "Richthofen" emblem and set of antlers. A Bf 109 can be seen in the background.*

Assi climbing out of his Bf 109 F-2, (Aircraft No. 6). Compare scraped looking area near the fuselage spine to other photos.

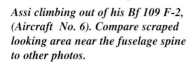

On the Yellow rudder of this new F machine are recorded 31 victory bars (even allowing for the discrepancy over his Hurricane claim on 14 May 1940, not officially credited), the date would be after 10 July 1941. This is the famous all-Yellow painted cowling aircraft embellished with the new version of Assi Hahn's rooster head emblem. Warm colors such as Yellow cause certain films like orthochromatic to appear very dark and was interpreted in post war years by some to be Red. This caused years of controversy and misunderstanding among artists, historians and enthusiasts even to this day.

Fuel was added to this fire when the excellent Profile Publications #184 written about the Bf 109 F by Martin Windrow published in 1967 featured an illustration inside the front cover of this Bf 109 F-2 of Assi Hahn's with a Red engine cowling and Red rudder. We now know, of course, these were Yellow. (Refer to color reference chart, Aircraft No. 5)

The identification marking used by the III. *Gruppe* on the early Bf 109 E types was the large *Welle* (wavy line) behind the fuselage cross. With the introduction of the new Bf 109 F type, the *Welle* was replaced by the vertical bar. Assi's Bf 109 F-2 appears to have initially used this third *Gruppe* vertical bar (the only photo known to the author is non-conclusive).

Photos of his next machine appear to be the same Bf 109 F-2 but now partially repainted; however, this new F-2 could be a different machine as so far the photos do not show the *Werknummer* clearly. The all-Yellow cowling has now been reduced to just the under portion and the Yellow rudder has 31 victory bars in a new, more elaborate design of White bars trimmed with Black featuring appropriate British and French Roundels.

The White command *Winkel* (Chevron) with a White triangle remains while the vertical III. *Gruppe* bar is now been replaced by a sporty, narrow White band, trimmed with Black, encircling the rear fuselage.

*Photos designated with a camera icon are from a rare home film and although of poor quality, are included here due to their historical significance. Here is the overall view of Assi's Bf 109 F-2, believed to be the same machine with the all-Yellow cowling but now partially re-painted reducing the Yellow to the undercowling only and converting the standard III. **Gruppe** vertical bar to the White band encircling the rear fuselage. The 31 victory bars are also now more elaborate, decorated with the roundels of the enemy aircraft. The White spinner has a RLM 70 Black-Green section. St. Pol, France July 1941. (Aircraft No. 6)*

 Assi's streamlined rooster head emblem, the Black area around the exhaust and White portion of the spinner are worth noting in this image.

The JG 2 "Richthofen" emblem has been removed from the fuselage, note the area just to the left of the mechanic.

Note the appearance of over spraying behind the White band, also a more narrow command chevron that is the same style used later on Assi's Bf 109 F-4.

The Black wing root and the C-3 96 octane fuel triangle indicative of a Bf 109 F-2 are of interest.

The Yellow rudder and the new style victory bars are clear, but unfortunately the Werknummer cannot be read. Because of this, it cannot be completely verified that this is the same aircraft as Assi's previous Bf 109 F-2 W. Nr. 5749.

The next known personal aircraft of Assi Hahn's was a Bf 109 F-4 *Werknummer* 7183[2], certified an F-4 by the revealing fuel triangle on the fuselage requiring an 87 octane rating as required by the F-4 subtypes. This machine is well-documented photographically while the unit was stationed at Saint Pol, France after Assi Hahn was awarded the Oak Leaves to his Knight's Cross on 14 August 1941. Similarly marked to his previous F-2, but now 46 victory bars are on the Yellow rudder, placing the date at late August 1941.

In a story published in the Zerbst *Stadtnachrichten* newspaper dated 6 September 1941, after the Presentation of the Oak Leaves to his *Ritterkreuz*, on 14 August 1941, Hptm. Hahn talks to the *"Mitteldeutsche"* about his missions against England. Here is that story:

"We remembered him exactly in this way: Tanned, vibrant and always full of good humor. We also recalled him from an event he had arranged for the *Winterhilfswerk* (Winter Support Organization) dancing as a temple dancer. This was Assi Hahn, the dashing pilot officer ready for any prank, who at one time literally flew on top of the audience onto a roof with his Fieseler *Storch* during a pilot get-together.

The Great Dane Lux, greeting his master as he consistently did after Assi returned from a mission. Note area where the JG 2 emblem has been over painted. (Aircraft No. 6).

Assi Hahn's Bf 109 F-2 with 31 victory bars on the Yellow rudder. The 31st victory was a Spitfire on 10 July 1941. This photo appears to have been taken at the same time the movie film was shot, frames of which are reproduced in this book. Assi Hahn can be seen sitting in the cockpit. (Aircraft No. 6)

"Yesterday we sat opposite him for half an hour at the "*Goldener Löwe*" (Golden Lion Hotel). Since we last saw him, he has been promoted to *Hauptmann*. On 5 October of last year, he was presented the *Ritterkreuz*[3] by the *Reichsmarschall*, and on Wednesday, *Hauptmann* Hahn was at the *Führerhauptquartier* where the *Führer* awarded him the Oak Leaves to the *Ritterkreuz* for his heroic work.

"*Hauptmann* Hahn was happy to meet old acquaintances. His former stomping grounds are very close to his heart, and the most wonderful peacetime memories are connected with the name of the town of Zerbst. He asked some old acquain-tances, party members Schmidt, Strinum and police *Leutnant* Fortnagel, who were also at the "*Löwe*," to join us at the table. Then he told us, upon our repeated request, about his missions against England.

"Time was short. During his last travel preparations *Hauptmann* Hahn recounted his 17th victory.[4] He was hunting over the island at that time. He was involved in a wild dogfight until one of the enemies was shot down and exploded above ground. Then the successful *Jagdflieger* discovered that the airbase Croydon was below him where the enemy was massed. But Assi returned safely to his airfield."

Right; Diethelm von Eichel-Streiber arrived to fly with Egon Mayer in 7. **Staffel***, early July 1941. The Iron Cross I Class seen on his jacket was awarded to him on 28 May 1941. He eventually was awarded the Knight's Cross on 5 April 1944. Serving in many different units he ultimately scored 96 credited victories.*

Left; Assi, Diet von Eichel-Streiber and Werner Stöcklemann enjoying a glass of wine in the III. **Gruppe** *headquarters building at St. Pol. Diet held Assi Hahn in the highest regard and believed he was one of the best fighter pilots and leaders he had ever known.*

Left; Egon Mayer taxies his Bf 109 F-2 "White 7". Note the III. Gruppe vertical bar.

Right; Egon Mayer in the doorway of the Chateau St. Pol, France that was the head-quarters of III./JG 2. Photo taken in July 1941 before Mayer received his Knight's Cross on 1 August 1941.

Left; Oberstleutnant Harry von Bülow-Bothkamp Geschwaderkommodore of JG 2 "Richthofen". His Knight's Cross was awarded on 22 August 1940. Photo taken with Assi at the Chateau St. Pol, July 1941.

 *Left; Hptm. Hahn on a holiday enjoying the Paris skyline from the balcony of his hotel.*

 Dinner with his fellow officers at a Paris restaurant where Assi is enjoying one of his favorite meals - Lobster!

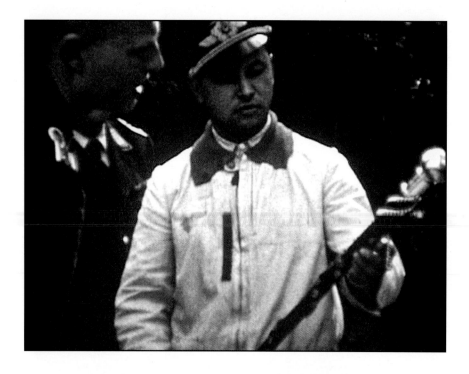

Left; Assi is admiring his new elaborate Abschußstock (Victory Stick) and command baton that has just been presented to him by a member of his staff. St. Pol, France, summer 1941.

Left; Assi proudly shows off his new victory stick to another officer.

Right; Hptm. Hahn at St. Pol, July 1941.

Hptm. Hahn on his Bf 109 F-4. He was awarded Oak Leaves to his Knight's Cross on 14 August 1941. Compare the point of the peak of the Black wing root with the photos of other III./JG 2 aircraft to help identify Hahn's aircraft. Then, note the absence of the "Richthofen" emblem, dropped in July 1941 for security reasons. (Aircraft No. 7).

A technician painting a White victory bar on the rudder of Hahn's Bf 109 F-4. Total of 46 victories, date 27 September 1941. Interesting points include the Yellow rudder with Gray camouflage area behind the bars, the victories over French aircraft (see victory list) bars numbered 4, 5 and 6, later changed to 3, 4 and 5. See photo No. 78, Fw 190); stencils on the trim tab elevator are clear, the paint thinner can and the small can of White paint. Is this officially RLM approved Weiss 21 or house paint? (Aircraft No. 7).

Close-up of Assi's Bf 109 F-4 tail, W. Nr. 7183, the all-Yellow rudder with 45 victories recorded. The 45th was a Spitfire on 20 September 1941. (Aircraft No. 7).

Assi and his beloved pet Great Dane "Lux" who was also a great favorite with the personnel of III./JG 2. Compare the camouflage mottling, plus size and position of Stab markings. (Aircraft No. 7).

This photo illustrates the upper camouflage pattern on the wing and stabilizer. (Aircraft No. 7).

*Lux with Assi who holds his beautiful Silver mounted **Abschußstock**, victory stick, presented to him by his unit. On the aircraft, note how different film type effects the roundels, compare with previous photos.*

Note the bottom row of victory bars applied directly over the Yellow rudder not over the Gray as the other rows.

Chapter 4 Notes:

1. W. Nr. 5749 built at Messerschmitt-Regensburg in March 1941, *Stammkennzeichen* KH + DN. It suffered 40% damage on 22 June 1941 with *Stab* JG 2 belly landing after combat at Arques airfield, France.

2. W. Nr. 7183 Bf 109 F-4 was built at the Wiener Neustädter factory. It was later turned over to III./JG 77 where it suffered 30% damage in an emergency landing on 15 January 1942.

3. *Ritterkreuz* was awarded on 24 September 1940, but presented on 5 October 1940.

4. Assi's 17th victory was a Hurricane on 11 September 1940 at 16:15, over Tournai, Belgium. However, the reporter is probably referring to the 20th a Spitfire that exploded over Croydon, England on 23 September 1940.

Chapter Five
A Visit by
Luftwaffe War Correspondent
Jochen Scheurmann

A story written about Assi Hahn and the III. *Gruppe* to be published in German newspapers and magazines about the progress of the war and successes of the unit is written by a visiting journalist. Bear in mind the purpose of this report is to encourage the German population to support the war effort.

Mission report 21
1 November 1941   *Kommandeur*

Soldiers and Pilots/The Best Fighters of the World

by War Correspondent Jochen Scheurmann

The runway looks deserted, only a few technicians are working on one of the machines. The other airplanes are standing lightly covered under their awnings, ready to start.
The *Kommandeur*, a medium sized, powerfully built *Hauptmann*, is talking to a *Leutnant* of his group. While speaking, a lock of his dark hair falls on his forehead which he ignores while continues conveying his orders.

At this moment, the alarm bells shrill: "*Alarmstart!*" The picture is changed within seconds; the calm that reigned over the airfield is transformed in a flurry of movement. The motors are started. The pilots are seated in their machines, and the *Kommandeur* is just now jumping into his Me 109 decorated with many victory markings on the rudder. Start! One machine after the other vanishes on the horizon.

But apparently the British fighter formation reported earlier has left, there is no Tommy in sight. The group has ascended to six thousand meters but cannot find any trace of the enemy. The ground posts also do not issue any new sightings. Turn back! They started once again in vane! Once

again the attackers withdrew earlier than the German pilots could be in position.

Ten Spitfires shoot at the Runway

In the same moment when the *Gruppenkommandeur* wants to issue the order for the return flight over the radio, he notices below, close to the ground, a few moving streaks.

Are these German or British machines? Surely, these are the Tommies!

In two wide swoops, the *Stabsschwarm* led by the *Gruppenkommandeur*, *Hauptmann* Hahn descend. They can now see clearly that these are ten Spitfires shooting with wild abandon at a small airfield. Again and again the machines turn and senselessly shoot at the runway, the barracks and the quarters of the airfield. It is not even occupied; maybe it is only a dummy airfield that the Tommies are stubbornly attacking.

"We'll show them," the men think in the machines descending from above, "We'll stop their fun!" Like hawks the four fighters dive down on the ten British planes. But the Tommies already noticed that danger is threatening.

Maybe one of the pilots, for a split second, averted his eyes from the barracks and hangars that they are riddling with bullets and glanced up there where the German airplanes approach. He must have been quite shocked because an attack started from high altitude is very difficult to deflect.

British discontinue circling around the airfield, and the narrow, slender Spitfires on whose wings the Germans can already discern the round blue-white-blue cockades are pulled around and try to flee across the Channel at high speed.

A Black Rooster at the Machines

But the Germans are already hard on their heels. A few of the Spitfires will get away with the German fighters catching the last four. They are somewhat at a distance from the other Tommies who are now fleeing in disarray; they are now the prey hunted by the fighter with the black rooster as the machine insignia. None of the four Spitfires will escape. It is as if the men of the *Stabsschwarm* had agreed on it. The British planes are soon in range; then the German salvos will shred their wings, their bodies, their motors. The first salvos will start now! The Tommies reach for their last weapon that could possibly save them still. They are trying to take advantage of the maneuverability of their machines.

After Wilhem Balthesar crashed to his death on 3 July 1941, Hptm. Walter Oesau took over JG 2 as the **Kommodore** *at the end of that same month. Oesau is shown here walking with Assi Hahn who is now the* **Kommandeur** *of III./JG 2 (29 October 1940).*

Fire over the Channel

The steep chalk cliffs are already ascending from the sea. It is time that they finally get to shoot, otherwise the British flak will thwart their efforts. The British seem to feel somewhat safer as they stop their dogfight and dash straight to the beckoning island. At the same moment, the *Kommandeur's* machine is behind the last Spitfire. A short salvo, then he sees that the British plane turns over forward and falls steeply downward. A large flame comes from the impact site in the sea. For a long time after the British machine submerged, the swimming oil is burning.[1] The other Spitfires turn to the right and want to resume the dogfight, but they are flying directly into the machine guns of the *Kommandeur's Rottenflieger*. Another British plane goes down, the remaining machines turn now to the left and into the gun of the German hunters. None of the British escapes. The four Messerschmitt machines are flying home wagging their wings.

Quite close to the beach of the northern French coast, they start a wild dogfight. The workers working barely ten meters below them at the barbed wire barriers throw themselves flat in the sand as if the machines would touch them. The British are fighting for their lives. They know that they would be lost if they flew straight to the island. In that instance the Me 109s would be again behind them and shoot them down one after the other. This is why they circle, roll and evade incessantly. They do not want to offer their pursuers a fixed target. It is pure aerial acrobatics that they are performing. But the Germans join in, they curve and circle as well as the Tommies. But they cannot avoid that they are slowly approaching the British coast.

"Lux" congratulating

The airplanes have barely taxied to a stop, the ground personnel men are there, open the cockpit canopy, congratulate and ask about the battle. A different congratulant is at the *Kommandeur's* machine.

Before the technicians and mechanic can reach the machine, a large black-and-white Great Dane runs with wide leaps toward his master's airplane. One Me 109 looks like the other, but "Lux" has never approached the wrong machine. The animal stretches up at the body and allows himself to be petted. Then the men of the group arrive and congratulate the *Kommandeur*.

While still seated in the machine or on the runway, Hptm. Hahn tells his adventures. He does this well, and one can discern from his men's faces how they follow every phase to the combat.

From a Piece of Wreck at Dunkerque

The *Jagdflieger*, in particular, is a single fighter. Maybe there is no other weapon where personal ability, own imitative and flexibility is as decisive as for the *Jagdfliegers*. The fighters share an exemplary comradeship. Not only among the *Jagdfliegers* themselves who, regardless of their rank, live together from the early morning to late at night but also among the pilots and the ground personnel. Just like the men in their black, oily denims who are maintaining and grooming the machines day in and day out and are standing restlessly and tensely on the runway and waiting for the return of "their" machine from the enemy mission, the fighters are equally concerned about their mechanics.

A nice example of this is the *Kommandeur's* walking stick. He always has the walking stick with him; there is no occasion when the "Old One" is seen without his stick. Indeed, it is a splendid specimen, this walking stick. A hand carved snake winds around the stick. On this snake, and recently also in the gaps, a number of highly polished five centime pieces are screwed onto the stick.

In Dunkerque, when the British armies were chased into the sea, the *Kommandeur's* leading mechanic found this stick. It had been brought ashore together with many other pieces of wrecks. Since then, a new five centime piece is added for each victory.

Never resting

The planes on the runway have been made ready for the start. New munitions, new fuel have been loaded, and the mechanics have thoroughly inspected the motors. The pilots of the *Stabs-*

schwarm are seated in the small pavilion at the runway edge. They are exchanging combat experiences.

When the group was transferred to this location a while ago, one of the first commands issued by the *Kommandeur* was the construction of this small house. Around it are wide, bright windows, only the rear wall is closed and has a beautiful fireplace where an open fire is kept going at all times. Only when it is cozily warm from the flaming beech wood logs, the *Hauptmann* feels well.

Now he is sitting together with his pilots waiting for the next mission. It is part of a *Jadgflieger's* destiny that there is never any rest for him; his *Staffel* or his *Schwarm* can be alarmed at any time and he must be ready to start so that machines can climb up in the air a few minutes later. They are sitting

*Icko the donkey, Assi and Lux the Great Dane,
St. Pol, Autumn 1941.*

Lux and "Wumm", a bear given to Assi by the Berlin Zoo, playing in front of Assi, Bruno Stolle and Josef Puchinger, officer on right not known. Autumn 1941, St. Pol.

and many a man who tried a wrestling match with him lost. Wumm would kick him down in one fell swoop and then run happily to the next man. The group almost has a complete zoo which is not surprising considering the *Kommandeur's* love for animals. Somebody once related that Assi Hahn dreamt as a boy to be a forest animal warden because he loved animals so much.

Down at the Chateau where the fighter pilots are quartered among a beautiful deciduous tree forest, the *Hauptmann* keeps another bunch of animals. First there is "Icko," the gray donkey and then also "Moritz," the large eagle-owl. But during the last few days, Moritz has fallen somewhat in disgrace. He was mean to the pretty golden pheasant. In a war-like moment, Moritz plucked out the pheasant's feathers one after the other. The mistreated pheasant died. Since then, the *Kommandeur* is angry with Moritz who knows this very well. Whenever the *Hauptmann* passes by his cage, he looks shyly aside as if he has a guilty conscience.

in the small house, dressed in their thick fur jackets with the swim vest over that. There is no billiard game here, otherwise the *Kommandeur* would surely play. Each of the men thinks his own thoughts, some converse, one reads and one is playing with the dog. They will only need to remain at readiness for a short while because now dusk is settling over the airfield.

"Moritz" is plucked

The Great Dane is lying next to the *Hauptmann*, sometimes he seems to sleep, another time he lifts his ears and look out with bright alertness when a motor is starting noisily. The *Kommandeur* goes out and looks after the small brown bear "Wumm" in his cage next to the command post. The bear is a present of the Berlin Zoo to the group, and Wumm has no complaints about the fighter pilots. He has been the darling of the all the men. Often, they play with him for hours on the runway. But Wumm is strong, as small as he is

(F) The Uhu (Eagle Owl) "Moritz" at the animal compound at St. Pol, France.

More than a hundred Enemy Missions

On this day, there will be no more alarms. It is now dark. In the Chateau, the pilots of the group are sitting together. One talks about his first enemy mission. It is long ago when the Hurricanes and Spitfires first appeared before these men. How many flights, how many hours of the hardest missions, how many desperate moments have occurred since

L to R, Werner Stöckelmann, Assi Hahn Gruppenkommandeur III./JG 2, and an unknown pilot, watch Lux and Wumm playing, St. Pol, France, Summer 1941.

then? Sometimes it seems an eternity! Almost all pilots of the *Stabsschwarm* wear the golden *Frontflug-Spange*[2] (combat clasp) which indicates more than one hundred enemy missions. Almost all wear the EK I, (Iron Cross First Class) some even the *Ritterkreuz*. The *Kommandeur* himself wears the Oak Leaves to the *Ritterkreuz*; he is at the top of the victory list of the group with his fifty victories.

I can rely on my Machine!

"Certainly, there were numerous tight moments but I always got out alright. I can rely on my machine one hundred percent, and I am not so bad a flyer. One only is excited and nervous as long as one cannot see the opponent. Once I have the enemy in front of me I am completely calm. Then I attack him cool as a cucumber. Why should I rush; I have time. First I get into the most favorable position and start my attack from there. I never underestimate my enemy but I also do not overestimate him."

Lux, the Great Dane got up. He moved to the window, loudly hitting the floor with his large paws. The pilots also got up to play a game of billiards. There is no word about flying and war. It appears as if a number of civilians is playing. Only the uniforms, the leather trousers and the fur boots are a reminder that these same men who now laugh and play without a care in the world are otherwise involved in a great battle. Each of them has been here at the Channel coast from the very beginning. Each of them has encountered the enemy many times and has started often against British fighters and heavy fighting machines.

Although a pet, a bear the size of Wumm is powerful and can be aggressive, Assi was one of the few who could compete successfully with Wumm perhaps because Assi was his trainer, but also due to Assi's powerful build and athletic ability.

Often published photo of a III./JG 2 Bf 109 F-4 illustrating the Hahn (rooster) emblem of Assi's III. Gruppe and the Yellow undercowl. This is not a known Hahn aircraft, note the position of the rooster head and the Black exhaust area.
                                                                    Bundesarchiv photo

The Air War at the Channel has been won

Ever since the beginning of the Russian campaign this group as well as other *Geschwadern* located here at the Channel have been embroiled in a bitter war against the British Air Force. It is thanks to these men that the British soon had to realize the uselessness of their attacks and now try to fly in only on rare occasions.

The men of this *Jagdgruppe* III./JG 2, have shot down one hundred and sixty British airplanes since June of this year at the northern French coast or over the Channel. This is a convincing proof of their superior flying prowess, their bravery as well as of the better performance of the German machines.

As everywhere, where men are fighting, this group also had is losses. Several pilots did not return from enemy missions. The comrades stood for a long time waiting on the runway and looked up full of hope that the missing Me 109 would show up. It did not come. Somewhere on the Channel a German soldier was claimed by his fate. But they did not slack, they started again and again, and fought against the Tommy until they finally can say: The aerial war over the channel is won, we are the victors! But they do not say that. Big words are not their cup of tea.

They perform their duties without words. They do not like to talk about their adventures; only when they are among each other, their reticence fades and then, during a quiet hour, they discuss the individual experiences. Today was such a day; today they told each other their adventure for the first time after a long interval. Sometimes, one interrupted the other or reported how he had seen the events when he was the *Rotte* comrade.

Eight Spitfires after me

One of the most desperate situations the *Kommandeur* ever experienced was during the attack of a larger British fighter formation.

"I was flying a bit lower than the British," the *Hauptmann* starts, "this made it possible for the British to turn toward me. And before I could take a breath, the whole gang was behind me. I had shot down one of them, but in that moment, the whole bunch was aligned as in a chain behind my Me 109. It may have been a whole squadron that flew closely after me. What could I do?

First I thought I could easily shake the Tommies off! I turned my machine on its head and dived down. They would hardly follow me in this manner! You can hardly imagine my shock, when I saw, upon a short glance to the rear, eight Spitfires behind me diving down as I did. And there they already started to fire

I felt very uncomfortable when the tracers of their shots flew outside the canopy right and left around my ears. With all their guns firing it is still a miracle that my plane was not made a sieve. But in my fear I must have automatically done the right thing. I curved and danced in an irregular manner through the area so that I simply could

The same aircraft as in the previous photo, shown under a wooden shed. The Black exhaust area on the peak of the wing root area is different than Assi's known aircraft; however it does have **Stab** *markings.   Bundesarchiv photo*

An armorer loading belted 20 mm cannon ammunition into Hahn's aircraft (Aircraft No. 7).   Bundesarchiv photo

A crew chief and technicians pose for the camera with Bf 109 F-4 W. Nr. 7183, one of Assi's aircraft, note position of the rooster head and mottling. Compare to two previous photos. (Aircraft No. 7)
Bundesarchiv photo

not be hit. Despite this, the British stayed hard behind me. We dashed along the coast at low altitude and then still lower over land. We barely missed at a whore's altitude (low altitude) the large memorial for the Canadians fallen in World War I. We curved hard around church steeples and houses, but the Spitfires still stayed behind me. Always when I believed that I had successfully shaken them off, more shots exploded around me.

Aerial Acrobatics for Life

It was a terrible dogfight that I was involved in for I was flying for my life. I used all my tricks and aerial acrobatics to shake the British pursuing me.

Rolls, turns, loops – all were useless. Like a wild chase, the eight Spitfires were after me. Their machine guns issued almost without interruptions severe salvos against my machine. It was my luck that our flight direction went above the countryside.

If I could hold out for a while, the British had to leave me because sometime their fuel must come to an end. And indeed, in the middle of a daring turn, I saw that the eight planes turned away and flew off.

But I was at the end of my strength. I could not have continued this wild dogfight and this wild chase for any length of time. Then I would have become the target of the British machine guns after all. Incidentally, I had not one single hit in the machine. First I did not want to believe it myself, but not one single shot could be found. The Tommies must have been damned bad shots."

The *Hauptmann* has finished his narrative; he gets up and says good night. The other pilots follow soon because they have to start early in the morning, and it is always better when one has slept well, than climbing into the machine as a tired man.

Only five hundred Kilometers per Hour

One or the other of the pilots must have thought, "The Old One is a snazzy guy!" Maybe they did not even think of the *Kommandeur's* many adventures or the many aerial victories. Maybe they only thought of the cheerful, friendly hours the group spent together. Who can forget the funny Thalia theater the boss is performing or his presentation of the old *Oberst* Hahn who long after the war will tell young people of his experiences: "Yes, yes, we had to be content with only five hundred kilometers per hour at that time. Just imagine that!"

This is how they are, the fighter pilots. This is how these men are who have to fight for their lives every day again and again. Some people may wonder that here are no cramped faces, no overly serious, embittered men but young officers and soldiers who know how to fight tenaciously and hard, but who can also be vivacious and high spirited.

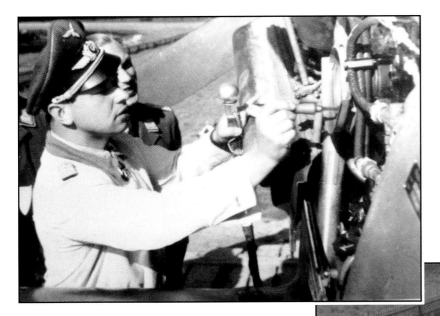

With Werner Stöckelmann looking on, Assi pokes a screw driver into the supercharger of his Bf 109 F for the camera. August 1941, St. Pol, France. (Aircraft No. 7)

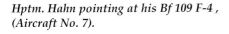

Hptm. Hahn pointing at his Bf 109 F-4, (Aircraft No. 7).

Technicians pushing Hahn's Bf 109 F-4 W. Nr. 7183 into a shed-type hangar. Note FuG 25 a antenna next to the mechanic on the right. (Aircraft No. 7)   Bundesarchiv photo

Mechanics arming Assi's Bf 109 F-4 W. Nr. 7183. Note 87 octane fuel triangle used by the F-4 subtypes. Compare camouflage pattern to other photos of Hahn's aircraft. (Aircraft No. 7)
                                                                                    Bundesarchiv photo.

Right; Werner Stöcklemann took over as Assi's wingman after the departure of Julius Meimberg on 1 August 1941. In the background is the Gefechtsstand (head-quarters) of III./JG 2. The 8. and 7. Staffel emblems can be seen on the edge of the roof. St. Pol, France, summer 1941.

Oblt. Werner Stöckelmann, III./ JG 2 adjutant and flew as Assi's wingman at times after the departure of Julius Meimberg on 1 August 1941. During a flight in an Fw 190 W. Nr. 0248, he failed to pull out of a dive, crashing to his death.

Above the London Airfield Croydon

Often the very pilot who looked into death's eyes a few hours earlier is the funniest among his comrades. How was that with the *Kommandeur*? In the middle of a dogged aerial combat, when he finally succeeded in shooting down his enemy, the *Hauptmann* noticed that he had been doing his dogfight smack over the large London airfield Croydon.

The Tommy machine that is crashing down burning fell right into the middle of many start ready Hurricanes and Spitfires down there. He pulled up his machine with a slight feeling of uneasiness.

How easy would it have been for the many fighter machines standing down there on the runway to get him down! How easily could the flak have dissected him into atoms. The flak must have seen him coming out of the clouds. But he made it! He pulled up rapidly and vanished in the cloud cover. Soon after landing he was again as always. Laughing, as if nothing had happened, he told his mechanics of his visit at Croydon and grand sight when the Tommy fell with a great splash in the middle of the of British fighters lined up in front of the hangars.

In the evening he played a funny radio show to amuse all men of his group. He narrated an imaginary ice hockey game like an old radio reporter. They all laughed uproariously, the thing was so very funny. Nobody considered that this man who was playacting so lively had returned only a short while ago from one of his most dangerous and difficult flights. (23 September 1940)

The best *Jagdflieger* in the World

When thinking of the German *Jagdflieger*, when talking about the men who fight against British pilots in their small, narrow machines high up in the air, one should not forget the human and well-balanced side of their soldier's life besides their hard, tough and warlike side. Especially the fighter pilots here at the Channel coast have shown that they are tough guys who can withstand any British attack.

Serious, hard fighters and still happy people who enjoy life, that's how our flyers are! Here at the Channel as well as in the huge country of Russia as well as at all war theaters, they have shown themselves as the best *Jagdfliegers* in the world. Nobody can dispute this rank!

In combat of man against man, they have proven themselves a thousand times as the best and superior. A grim, tough enemy is opposing them, but they have shown that they are able to fly and fight still harder, still tougher, and still bolder. They can always be proud of their successes.

War Correspondent Jochen Scheurmann

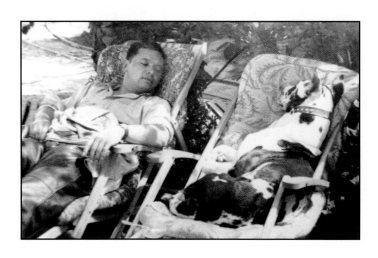

A moment of rest for Lux and his owner.

Gruppenkommandeur *Hahn's* Stab *Major Oblt. Josef Puchinger's striking Bf 109 F-4
undergoing fueling as Puchinger is pointing at his victory bars on the rudder. FuG 25 a
antenna barely visible under* Stab *markings.*

Oblt. Puchinger posing with his technicians in front of his Bf 109 F-4.

*Hptm. Hahn in White jacket with members of his III. Gruppe. Egon Mayer awarded the Knight's Cross on 1 August 1941 and **Staffelkapitän** 7. **Staffel**; Assi; Bruno Stolle **Staffelkapitän** 8. **Staffel**, he would receive his Knight's Cross on 17 March 1943; Werner Stöckelmann, 9. **Staffel**, KIA flying an Fw 190 W. Nr. 0248 failing to pull out of a dive on 29 May 1942; right, unknown. Behind the group is Assi's Bf 109 F-4 (Aircraft No. 7).*

*Oblt. Josef Puchinger of **Stab** III./ JG 2 in front of his Bf 109 F-4. Note position of the rooster head.*

*Below; Possibly the same **Stab** machine on pages 66 and 67. Note the position of the rooster head and style of Black wing root area.*

No doubt the III. Gruppenstab will dine very well this night.

A very happy **Gruppenkommandeur** *Hptm. Hahn proudly showing off his beautiful silver-mounted* **Abschußstock,** *victory stick, presented to him by his staff. On the right is Oblt. Werner Stöckelmann, to the left out of the picture, is Hahn's* **Stab Major Oblt. Josef Puchinger,** *Fall 1941, St. Pol, France.*

A pensive moment between Lux and Assi.

Very casually dressed without his Knight's Cross, Assi walks with Oblt. Werner Stöckelmann. Note the nose of the Bf 109 F in the hangar.

Staffelkapitän *Bruno Stolle 8./JG 2 in his "Black 12" Bf 109 F admires a trophy Spitfire wheel dated 23 July 1941.*

Below; An unidentified Bf 109 F with **Stab** *markings. Note the lock on the aileron.*

 The American auto used by Assi as his personal Staff Car, note the command pennant on the fender and the small JG 2 emblem on the door.

The ever-present Great Dane, Lux in front of a military motorcycle escorting the unit's move to a new location. Note what appears to be a Fokker Triplane painted on the sidecar.

Trucks moving some of the heavy equipment needed to support the aircraft.

L to R, Oblt. Puchinger Stab Major holding Assi's victory stick, Oblt. Egon Mayer and Hptm. Assi Hahn, who appears to be looking at his camera, late 1941, Cherbourg, France.

Oblt. Werner Stöckelmann taking photos of a group of officers including Puchinger, on the left, next to him an Army officer and Assi with his head tilted, late 1941, Cherbourg, France.

The dramatic French coastline at Felsentor, near Etretat where Assi Hahn, on a dare, confident of his skill and flying ability, rolled his aircraft over into a 90 degree bank and flew through the opening in the cliff. Only he could get away with this!

Although difficult to see in the harsh light captured in this image, Assi Hahn's rudder on his Bf 109 F-4 at this time displays 50 victory bars, 13 October 1941. (Aircraft No. 7)

Left; Oblt. Erich Leie leaning on a propeller blade of a Bf 109 F-4 of the JG 2 Geschwaderstab. He recieved his Knight's Cross on 1 August 1941.
Bundesarchiv photo

Facing page, top photo; **Major Oesau** *in another one of his Bf 109 F-4s with Komodore's markings. Note evidence of earlier chevron markings behind the rather small command chevron and bar. Of note also is the 87 octane fuel triangle outlined in Black instead of the usual White outline. The machine appears to have been recently re-camouflaged indicated by the factory data plate that has been over painted.*

Bundesarchiv photo

Left; **Major Walter Oesau** *the* **Kommodore** *of JG 2 since the end of July, 1941 climbing out of one of his Bf 109 F-4 after a mission. He ventually would achieve 127 victories and be awarded the Swords and Oak Leaves to his Knight's Cross.*

Left; Major Oesau appearing to be removing his Schwimmweste after a flight. Note the flares on the rear fuselage and the pistol on the stabilizer. Note too, the White-walled tail wheel.

Bundesarchiv photo

Four images of "Yellow 9" Bf 109 F-2 W. Nr. 9553 flown by **Staffelkapitän** Oblt. Siegfried Schnell 9./JG 2. On 8 November 1941 Schnell had an important day downing three Spitfires, bringing his total to 57 victories, recorded on his Yellow rudder.

Some F-2s were upgraded by retrofitting DB 601 E engines as they became available, to the existing airframe. These aircraft can be recognized by the new 87 octane fuel triangle on the port side of the fuselage, replacing the old F-2 requirement of C 3 fuel. The 87 octane fuel triangle can be seen in other photos of this aircraft.

The White side wall tire can be seen in several of these photos. Photos showing the starboard side of Schnell's "Yellow 9" reveal paint on the Yellow rudder having extensive peeling.

"Yellow 1" and "Yellow 2" of 9./JG 2 can be seen in the background. Note the new camouflage over the previous all-yellow cowlings.

Two technicians carrying linked ammunition in front of Schnell's "Yellow 9".

Oblt. Rudolf Planz, a member of the Geschwaderstab is showing a female nurse a Bf 109 F-4 Stab aircraft. On the wing is Günther Seeger, left and Oblt. Erich Leie. This machine is marked with a bar, rectangle above and another bar to the rear of the fuselage cross.

*"White 1" Bf 109 F-4 of Egon Mayer, **Staffelkapitän** of 7./JG 2. Note the **Kapitän's** pennant with the 7. **Staffel** emblem on the antenna mast. This machine is similar to his earlier Bf 109 F-2 "White 1", W. Nr. 6720 that displayed 23 victory bars on the rudder. Mayer received the Knight's Cross after his 21st victory on 1 August 1941. Photos of this F-4 show the trees in the background without their leaves indicating late 1941.*

Egon Mayer, wearing his Knight's Cross, climbing into his "White 1". Note the overhead armor installed in the canopy.

Chapter 5 Notes:

1. Reporter referring to Assi's 50th victory on 13 October 1941 at 14:30.

2. Bronze clasp was presented after 20 operational flights, Silver after 60, Gold after 110.

Chapter Six
Changes

III. Gruppenkommandeur Hahn's Fw 190 A-2, W.Nr. 223 with 61 victories recorded on the Yellow rudder. Of interest, the date of his 61st and 62nd victories is 6 May 1942. (see victory list) Beaumont le Roger, France, May 1942. (Aircraft No. 8)

*Close-up of the victory bars on the Yellow rudder of Assi Hahns Fw 190 A-2 W. Nr. 223.
Note the 3rd, 4th and 5th, now reflect the correct French victories.*

Beginning in May 1942, Assi's III. Gruppe began to re-equip with the Focke-Wulf 190. This one is the famous A-3 W.Nr. 5313 that Oblt. Armin Faber inadvertently delivered to the RAF on 23 June 1942. Note the fuselage behind the exhaust was painted Black before Faber's infamous flight, see photo below. (Aircraft No. 9)

To supplement the Luftwaffe's aging fighter, the Messerschmitt Bf 109, a new type of aircraft was beginning to make its presence known, the radial-engine Focke-Wulf 190. Modern engineering included all-electrical systems and wide track landing gear to help counter the constant problem of accidents occurring with the narrow landing gear of the 109. However, teething problems plagued the air-cooled BMW 801 radial engine with over-heating resulting in fires.

A twelve-bladed fan plus fuselage cooling vents helped to overcome this problem. That and other bugs associated with a new design were eventually worked out. Ultimately the result was a medium altitude fighter that was superior to any opponent it met, at the time.

First introduced to the other *Jagdgeschwader* on the Channel front, JG 26, a year earlier, Assi's III./JG 2, now stationed at Cherbourg/Théville, a beautiful Chateau with meadow airfields and plush grounds, where they received their first Fw 190s in May 1942 when 35 A-2 sub-types were delivered directly from the manufacturer.

Aerial success continued for Assi Hahn achieving a total 66[1] victories by 16 September 1942, all of them single engine fighters!

Assi dismounting Fw 190 A-3 W. Nr. 5313 also pictured in above photo. Black paint not yet applied on the fuselage.

One of Assi's many friends from other branches of service, this **Wermacht** officer poses in front of one of Assi's Fw 190s. Note his riding boots with spurs. In this photo, the Yellow undercowling appears light

Below; The same visiting **Wermacht** officer sits in the cockpit of one of Assi's Fw 190s. The Black exhaust area cowling bumps and the fuel octane triangle requiring C 3 100 octane fuel are visible.

Right; an unidentified lady friend in the cockpit of Assi's Fw 190. The early style head armor with the 'long neck' is just visible.

Below; The camera-shy lady friend with the visiting officer, in front of Assi's Fw 190. The White III. Gruppe band can be seen. The camouflage closely matches W. Nr. 5313 that Faber inadvertently landed in England.

Showing visitors the unit's Fw 190s; the Yellow under cowl in the photograph appears dark due to the film type. Also note the Black exhaust area.

*"White 1" Fw 190 A-4 W. Nr. 2413 of Obfw. Kurt Knappe of 7./JG 2. Knappe was awarded the Knight's Cross on 3 November 1942 after achieving 51 victories serving with JG 51 in Russia. He was transferred late November 1942 to 7./JG 2 and was killed on 3 September 1943. Notable is the Yellow undercowl and lighter Yellow rudder with 52 White bars, 51 with Russian stars and one with an RAF roundel. Here the vertical bar is used for the III./ **Gruppe** identification along with the Rooster head on the cowling. Black exhaust area is typical. The portable power supply is connected to the socket in the **Balkenkreuz** preparing to start the engine.*

*"White 5" Fw 190 A-2 W. Nr. 5266 of 7./JG 2. This colorful aircraft has Yellow rudder and undercowling, Black exhaust area and on the cowling is the emblem of 7. **Staffel**. In the right background, "White 8" is the aircraft of Lt. Jakob Augustin.*

Obfw. Sepp Keil of JG 2, sitting in a Fw 190 "Yellow 8" with the nickname Luki-Luki. Note the early style pilot's headrest and the unique double bracing typical of the A-1 sub-type.

Right; An Army officer looking at an Fw 190 from III./JG 2. It appears the MG 17s have been obliterated from the photo. The open supercharger scoop can be seen just above the wheel.

Below; A Stab Fw 190 A-4 marked like Assi's aircraft but is Egon Mayer's, Assi's successor as **Kommandeur** *of III./JG 2. Note the supercharger scoop to aid in high altitude performance.*

Two views of Obslt. Oesau's Fw 190 A-5 W. Nr. 1230, "Green 13" taken at Beaumont-le-Roger, France June 1943. The top photo shows no victory markings on the Yellow rudder. The bottom photo has five victories recorded as drawings of four-engined bombers, numbers 101 -105. Detail of the five bomber victory markings on the rudder can be seen to the left; note two show bombers caught fire. These were his last victories as **Kommodore** *of JG 2, as he left on 1 July 1943.*

Later, while **Kommodore** *of JG 1, he was killed on 11 May 1944.*

A drastic change occurred in Assi's career on 1 November 1942. He was requested by the *Kommodore* of JG 54 *"Grünherz"* (Green Hearts) *Oberstleutnant* Hannes Trautloft, an old friend aware of Assi's leadership qualities, to take command of II./JG 54 at the large air field Rjelbitzy (Rjelbitzi) south of Lenningrad, (St. Petersburg) Soviet Union. Hptm. Hahn would have big shoes to fill, taking over for the quiet, gentle, professional leader *Oberstleutnant* Dietrich Hrabak, who commanded this unit since August 1940. Leaving to take over as *Kommodore* of JG 52 Hrabak's last flight as a member of Green Hearts was on 26 October 1942, flying a Bf 109 G-2 W. Nr. 10376.[2]

Extreme adjustment was required for the new *Kommandeur*, used to the comfortable French Chateau lifestyle, to his new environment now a harsh, bitterly cold winter atmosphere with limited creature comforts. One of the few pleasures the pilots were able to enjoy was the popular sauna at Rjelbitzy.[3] The Russian air force was becoming more and more formidable, with better training and improved aircraft designs; it was no longer a turkey shoot as it was in June 1941.

To this new unit, Assi brought with him his charismatic leadership and sense of humor. Assi settled in quickly, gaining the confidence of his men who referred to him as *Vater* or father, which was also his radio identification name. He was now flying the newer and more powerful Messerschmitt Bf 109 G-2. Rapidly his score increased to include three Ilyushin Il 2s, the hard-to-kill "Cement Bombers"[4], which he downed on 4 December 1942. On the same day, he also scored a LaGG 3 fighter.

Starting the new year, Assi Hahn was promoted to *Major* on 1 January 1943. His most successful day ever was on 14 January when he managed to knock down an incredible seven of the Soviet's best aircraft, at that time, the Lavochkin La 5, three of these in three minutes.

JG 54 had a tradition of using an unusual non-standard command chevron for its *Stab* machines. This version of the command chevron is seen on Assi's known Bf 109 G-2s. The first one, W. Nr. unknown, has a single chevron with narrow alternating borders of Black and White, with a similar design for the horizontal second *Gruppe* bar behind the fuselage cross.[5] Assi achieved his 100th victory claim flying this aircraft on 26 January 1943[6], a significant date for the unit as another of its *Experten* reached a milestone. After scoring five on this day, Lt. Max Stotz[7] brought his total to 150.

This series of rare photos is from a film taken in Russia of Gruppenkommandeur Major *Assi Hahn after a flight in his Bf 109 G-2. (Aircraft No. 10) Because of the poor quality they are printed small; nevertheless, they are presented here due to the historical significance.*

 This camera icon indicates image still from movie.

 Major Hahn climbing out of his Bf 109 G-2 (Aircraft No. 10)

 A better view of the canopy bulkhead as Major Hahn climbs down.

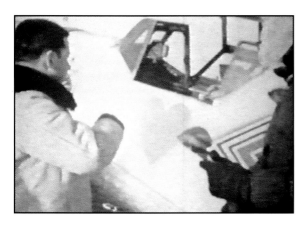

*A good view of the unusual command chevron of this **Stab** machine. The center portion appears to be a Dark gray, with alternating White borders and Black lines, and the outside edge Dark camouflage under White snow camouflage.*

*Assi speaking with Oblt. Hans Beißwenger, **Staffelkapitän** of 6./JG 54. Note the White overspray on the **Hakenkreuz**.*

Technician installing the camera in the cockpit with another mechanic sitting on the wing.

Another view of the large, unusual command chevron. The landing gear doors have been removed to prevent snow and ice from impacting, restricting movement.

*A technician preparing a camera to be mounted on the cannon cover in the cockpit, filming the pilot during a mission. This sequence was prepared for a flight of Hptm. Heinrich Jung, Assi's successor to II./JG 54. A small portion of the unusual II. **Gruppe** bar can be seen on the left.*

Assi's Bf 109 G-2 with the single chevron at right with its engine still running after landing.

IM NAMEN
DES DEUTSCHEN VOLKES
BEFÖRDERE ICH
DEN HAUPTMANN IN DER LUFTWAFFE
HANS HAHN
MIT WIRKUNG VOM 1. JANUAR 1943
ZUM MAJOR

ICH VOLLZIEHE DIESE URKUNDE IN DER ERWAR-
TUNG · DASS DER GENANNTE GETREU SEINEM
DIENSTEIDE SEINE BERUFSPFLICHTEN GEWIS-
SENHAFT ERFÜLLT UND DAS VERTRAUEN
RECHTFERTIGT · DAS IHM DURCH DIESE BEFÖR-
DERUNG BEWIESEN WIRD. ZUGLEICH SICHERE
ICH IHM MEINEN BESONDEREN SCHUTZ ZU.

FÜHRERHAUPTQUARTIER, 18. DEZEMBER 1942.

DER FÜHRER

Promotion certificate for Hans "Assi" Hahn from **Hauptmann** *to* **Major***, effective 1 Jaunary 1943.*

Now a **Major,** *promoted on 1 January 1943, Assi is being recognized for his 100th victory accomplished on 27 January 1943 over a Lagg 3. On the left is Lt. Max Stotz who flew as Hahn's wingman on many occasions. This is a double celebration as Stotz is being honored for achieving his 150th victory on 26 January. On the right is Oblt. Hans Beißwenger,* **Staffelkapitän** *of 6./JG 54. Interestingly Assi is still wearing his* **Jagdgeschwader "Richthofen"** *cuff title on his uniform sleeve.*

Assi's last known Bf 109 G-2, W. Nr. 13949, equipped with 20 mm cannon underwing gondolas, still marked on the underwing with its original factory *Stammkennzeichen* of DL HW wore the command double chevron and horizontal second *Gruppe* bar. This design was somewhat simplified from the previous aircraft, consisting of a Black chevron with a White border trimmed with a thin Black outline.[8]

1 November 1942, Assi Hahn was transferred from his beloved JG 2 **"Richthofen"** *and sent to Russia to take command of II./JG 54* **"Grünherz"** *(Green Hearts). Here he is in his Bf 109 G-2.*

*Now the **Gruppenkommandeur** of II./JG 54, photos document at least two different Bf 109 G-2s flown by Hahn. Pictured above and on the next page is his last known aircraft with the distinctive JG 54 type double chevron, W. Nr. 13949 **Stammkennzeichen** DL + HW (Aircraft No. 11). Compare this chevron to the one in photos on page 87, (Aircraft No. 10). This aircraft was equipped with 20 mm under wing cannon gondolas. Note the letter "H" under the port wing, the large JG 54 Green Heart, and the II. Gruppe Lion of Aspern on forward fuselage, located on both sides. Note too, the vertical bulkhead at rear of canopy with unusual flat overhead armor plate over pilot's head.*

In these two photos, a photographer is filming as Gruppenkommandeur Hahn taxis by in his Bf 109 G-2 W. Nr. 13949. (Aircraft No. 11)

Running up the engine of Assi's Bf 109 G-2 W. Nr. 13949, Rjelbitzy, Russia Winter 1942-1943. The RLM 70 Dark Green of the spinner is over sprayed with winter camouflage to lighten the color as is the Yellow under cowling. Note lower portions of landing gear doors removed to avoid snow impacting. Seldom seen in photos is the restrictor panel inside the oil cooler radiator cowling. This was used to help the engine run warmer in extremely cold conditions.

Right; Close-up of the restrictor panel, note the stenciling that reads "F und G".

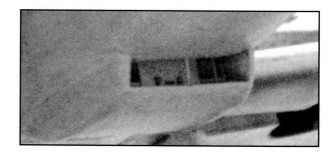

Chapter 6 Notes:

1. Although 68 victories were claimed, causing some confusion, 66 were officially confirmed. Hans Ring.
2. Dieter Hrabak's *Flugbuch*
3. Author's interview with General Hannes Trautloft and General Dietrich Hrabak, 1991.
4. Nicknamed by German pilots, "Cement Bomber" due to the heavily armored fuselage because it was like shooting at cement.
5. See photos and profile.
6. The actual date of his 100th officially credited victory was on 27 January 1943. Hans Ring.
7. Lt. Stotz flew many missions as Assi Hahn's wing man.
8. See photos and profile

Chapter Seven
Endings

On the very cold morning of Sunday 21 February 1943, circumstances arose that would change Major Assi Hahn's life forever ending his career as a flyer in the Luftwaffe. The following story is written in his own hand and was published in a book he wrote *"Ich Spreche die Wahrheit!"* (**"I Speak the Truth"**) that he dedicated to his friend Erich Hartmann who was still in captivity and would not be released until 1955. It is his story about his last mission, his capture by the Soviets and the inhumane treatment by them as a prisoner of war.

He praises some of his fellow captured German officers and damns others, but that's another story. This book was published in Germany by Bechte Verlag in 1951. Our excerpt is used by permission of Assi's widow, Gisela Hahn.

LAST FLIGHT AND IMPRISONMENT

By Assi Hahn

"Once in a while, fate gives a warning to a person who is facing a hard time so that he is not completely unprepared in his dark hour. I was not blessed with such a warning; on the contrary, the events overran me completely unexpectedly.

"It was Sunday, 21 February 1943. In the morning I left the command post with the intention to fly to Riga in order to arrange for my furlough besides some business matters at the *Luftflotte.* I was eager to have my one hundred fiftieth victory before that and then to have a few holidays with my wife at the Zugspitze, Germany's highest mountain.

"On this clear, very cold day – thirty-eight below zero degrees Celsius -- I gave no thought to a flight to the front and exchanged my usual fur combination with my old white sports pilot outfit. On the way to the runway, accompanied as always by my Great Dane Lux, my constant *Rotte* comrade Max Stotz[1] ran toward me and reported that there was unusually strong Russian flying activity in the area of Demiansk. The army was urgently requesting fighter support. The German troops were withdrawing during these days from the so-called "Demiansk belt" to move back to a new front line.

" 'These guys are getting too fresh and must be taught a thorough lesson.' Stotz said, leaving no room for a misunderstanding. Under these circumstances, my plan to fly to Riga had to be abandoned. Lux was tied to my walking stick lodged in the snow, as was usual in many other flights to the front, and had to wait for my return. It was always this faithful dog who greeted me first after each landing.

"I was just climbing in the parachute when my faithful old friend Alfons ran to the machine with an armful of mail and reported that a "Ju 52" had landed and delivered a lot of mail for me including four letters from my wife. 'Put them on my desk, Alfons, I will be back in forty-five minutes and look at them then...'

"On the dot of nine o'clock, the *Stabsschwarm* sat on the runway of Rjelbitzy, our small airfield in the northern section of the eastern front, stepped on the gas for the last time in this constellation and with the familiar drone of the motors we lifted from the ground. We gained altitude steadily and flew toward the Ilmen lake which we reached after ten minutes near Staraja-Russa. Our *Adlerwachen* (Eagle Watches) reported from the "belt" the location of many "Indians." This was our nickname for enemy fighters.

"Stotz who was flying fifty meters from me had discovered many black dots in the light blue sky above us with his eagle eyes. The dots danced wildly, and he made me aware of them. We had the Russians in front of us. Soon this exciting wild dance I loved so much and that was familiar from over France, the Channel, England and finally Russia, would begin anew. It was here, in comparison to the western front, so temptingly without danger, all the caution required over the Channel seemed superfluous here.

"Below us was land, terra firma, no water. We flew no higher than ten thousand meters altitude as our hunting area was at three thousand or below. The sea equipment such as life vest with pressured air bottle, life raft, flares and pistol and even oxygen mask that restrain the pilots was all absent and gave us a fabulous feeling of freedom of movement. There was this tremendous desire to fight in this elegant little Messerschmitt, to accept a challenge that had to end victorious. You or I – only one leaves the battlefield as the victor. Even when defending himself, a *Jagdflieger* had to attack. His weapons are built-in facing rigidly to the front, nobody shoots to the rear, and this is why his first commandment in aerial battle was: Get behind the enemy! The rest is then easy.

"The Russian state of training was far inferior to ours and that of the British. The enemies of the Messerschmitt here were not Spitfires but Airacobras and Laggs; in any event, I had been always the victor before, and that was the main factor for my feeling of superiority. Therefore, on to the enemy because he who is there first shoots first and wins.

"The dots increased in size and soon turned out to be fifty to sixty Airacobras I had a 'pointed nose' in front of me after the first moment. One hundred meters, seventy, fifty. Then a fire burst. In front of me a bright explosion, and the Russian is no longer there.

"Stotz who also was fighting announced over the radio: 'This one got his lesson.' After the first there is a second. But another one with a red star was behind me. His unwelcome volleys hit my left wing and came dangerously close to the cockpit.

"He had to be shaken off and punished. In the meantime, Stotz' first victory went down far left from me. After a few very pointedly flown figures, I got right of the Russian behind me but I noticed soon that I had an expert before me who made things extremely hard for me. The embittered air combat was close to the ground, slightly above the northern Russian primeval forest.

"It was hot in the Messerschmitt. The windows in the machine fogged up and I had to open them. Stotz reported just now his second victory which I could not see because we had moved too far apart when the Russian leveled his machine and tried to get away toward the east. I was in a favorable shooting position, released a short fire burst, the machine in front of me turned over and crashed with a huge flame into the forest. I was rid of him, thank God. [2]

"Because of the constant flight at full throttle, the oil temperature had increased to 'very high'. A smell of burned cables permeated the machine. Something was smoldering that was not supposed to smolder. Annoying! I was all alone, above and behind me were still thirty Russians! So I decided to fly toward the west as I had lost the orientation during the preceding battle and the forest looked alike everywhere. It was not clear if I was over our own or over enemy territory.

"When I took course to the west, I saw that two fighters were preparing to attack me from a higher altitude. I was alone, had very little ammunition left and a hot machine; therefore, I felt no desire to take up another battle. I gave up my last altitude and pressed my Messerschmitt directly over of the tree tops thinking I could shake off the Russians with this maneuver. A few seconds later, there was a hard bang that shook the whole machine. In the same moment the propeller stopped! Fearful silence.

"What now happened went very fast. The speedometer showed barely two hundred kilometers. The Messerschmitt would drop down. The oil temperature had reached the upper limit. This slow speed allowed no pulling up the machine in order to jump with the parachute. To stop on the trees with two hundred kilometers and dash into forest was also not a wise proposition. I had seen a fire-break on the left. If I could reach it, I could make a belly landing.

"I decided quickly, turned the machine with the side control by one hundred eighty degrees. Without giving up one meter altitude, I slipped through the remaining tree tops to the supposed fire-break which, however, turned out to be a street on which an endless column of fur clad figures marched in the direction from which I came.

"I was horrified. I gave my last words through the radio: 'Stotz, they taught Father a lesson, I must land'. I switched off the electrical system and landed with a speed of one hundred and fifty kilometers right next to the marching column. Then a shimming cloud of snow obscured everything, and finally the Me 109 was lying on its belly almost undamaged.

"When I opened the cabin, I was shot at from a thousand barrels from all weapons, or so it appeared. I reached behind me and put on my visored cap. This is how I climbed out of the cabin. Because the shooting did not stop and I did not yet understand that I was now a prisoner, I yelled: 'Stop!' and waved with my glove. The effect was surprising. I heard them yell 'General, General,' the shooting ceased, the soldiers ran toward me, pulled me off the cockpit edge, some in one direction and some in the other and pushed my arms up.

"The situation changed soon in that a good-looking Russian, with better fur clothes, came to me, beat the soldiers with a stick and drove me from the street into the forest. Two soldiers held my arms up. Between the trees I saw one bunker after the other. I was pushed into the first bunker. Two officers and a good-looking young girl also in uniform with a pistol sat under a weak light that spread a strange, earthy smell. While two pistols threatened me, the girl ordered me in accent-free German: 'Get undressed!'

"I began to take off my combination suit. When my shoulder pieces were revealed the interpreter said: 'Ah, you are an officer, undress faster, you fascist pig!' A minute later I stood stark naked with raised hands in front of the Russians. One of the officers took my wristwatch and my ring. The girl remarked that I would not need these things any longer. In this unpleasant circumstance, the first interrogation started.

'What is your name?'
'Hahn.'
'What is your rank?'
'Major.'
'Where is your pistol?'
'I have none. I want to tell you from the start that I will give you no further information.'

"The Russians looked at me furiously. 'We have the means to make the most silent people talkative. We will use these means on criminals like you. The Hauptmann asked me to tell you: When you do not answer you will be shot.'

"When I did not respond, the older officer cranked the field telephone. I heard several times 'Major Gan' during the conversation. After they had looked me over once more, they returned my underpants, combination jacket, cap, and *Ritterkreuz*.

"The rest was thrown in a corner of the bunker. It was clear to me that now came the last walk, that all would be over. For this reason, I did not worry about my inadequate clothing. I left the room with my arms up. When I left the bunker, more then fifteen soldiers pointed their guns at me. But no shot rang out. Flanked on both sides by Russians, an officer ordered me to go toward the street without looking back.

"We had left the forest by a few steps, and the soldiers stopped. The accompanying officer stayed behind and let me walk alone. Now, I thought, comes the famous shot in the neck! Involuntarily, I pulled my head in as soon it would all be over. I wonder of it hurts? But it was not over yet.

"After a few steps I had reached the street, still no shot. I was still alive. On the right was my machine. A Russian soldier sat in it and triumphantly showed his comrades the dismantled board clock. This was the last time I saw an Me 109."

A Soviet report of the incident when Assi Hahn was captured records the following:[3]

"On 21 February 1943, 6 VA (air army) reported seven aerial combats and 13 German aircraft shot down. During one of those air combats, 169 IAPs Starshiy Leytenant (Senior Lieutenant) Pavel Grazhdaninov and his wingman, Starshiy Serzhant Davydov, claimed to have shot down five Bf 109s.

"According to the Soviet combat report, one of the pilots who was shot down by Grazhdaninov bailed out over Soviet-controlled territory, and when he was captured it turned out that he was the commander of 'II. *Gruppe* of JG 54'. This of course was Hahn, and he was brought to a Soviet fighter base[4]. "The Soviet account continues: The captured German pilot was very brazen and stated that he had not been shot down, that his engine had suffered overheating: 'The pilot who can defeat me has not yet been born. I got three of yours today!' When Hahn's words had been translated, Polkovnik Storozhenko commented: 'What a boaster! We lost no more than a single plane today.' (Assi Hahn confirmed that he was brought to a Soviet fighter base, and that he had a similar discussion with a Hero of the Soviet Union.) Hahn flew Bf 109 G-2/R6, W. Nr. 13949, Black double chevron; Grazhdaninov flew a La-5.

Overall view of captured military vehicles and aircraft on display in Russia during the war. Bf 109 G-2 "Double Chevron", the aircraft Assi Hahn was flying when he was downed and captured, is third from the top. From this photo, it is obvious that he did not bail out as stated in the Russian report, rather he belly landed his aircraft behind enemy lines.

Chapter 7 Notes:

1. Max Stotz, 189 victories. Awarded the Knight's Cross on 19 June 1942 and the Oak Leaves on 30 October, 1942.
2. Assi's 108th credited victory, his last, was a La 5 at 0911 on 21 February 1943.
3. Correspondence with Historian and Author Christer Bergström 2002
4. Conflicting information here, as Assi Hahn did not bail out but rather belly landed. His Bf 109 G-2 was included in a display of captured German equipment and appeared to be in good condition. If he would have bailed out, of course, this aircraft would have been destroyed. The German loss records indicate only one Bf 109 lost in this area on this day.

Chapter Eight
Letters of Condolence

The following two letters were written to Assi Hahn's wife from JG 54 *Kommodore Oberstleutnant* Hannes Trautloft.

J.G. 54
KOMMODORE   Command Post, 22 February 1943

Dear esteemed Lady,

Unfortunately, I have to give you the sad news that your husband did not return on 21 February after his 108th aerial victory from an enemy mission in the area south of the Ilmen lake and that he has been missing since then. His regular *Rotte* comrade, *Leutnant* Stotz, an extremely experienced and reliable pilot, reports on the events of the aerial combat:

"I started on 21 February 1943 at 0855 hours as the *Rottenführer* with *Major* Hahn as the *Rotte* flyer to monitor the runway Demjansk[1] - Ramuschewo. At 09:09 hours, at the southern edge of the land bridge, we encountered the enemy with 8 Lagg-5s[2] at an altitude of 2500 meters. A *Schwarm* of Me 109's under the leadership of *Oberfeldwebel* Wefers participated in this battle. I and *Major* Hahn attacked a *Schwarm* of Lagg-5's flying 200 m below us. *Major* Hahn and I each shot down 1 Lagg-5 in this attack. During the developing air battle, I lost sight of *Major* Hahn. I tried to get in radio contact with *Major* Hahn, but this remained without success due to bad communication."

Another supplementary report was given by *Oberfeldwebel* Repple who flew as *Rottenführer* in the *Schwarm* of *Oberfeldwebel* Wefers. He reported: "At 09:10 hours, we encountered the enemy in the form of 8 Lagg-5's at an altitude of 2500 m. In the course of the developing aerial battle, I wanted to attack a Lagg-5 flying somewhat lower, but I saw that an Me 109 was already attacking the plane. I recognized the Me 109 as *Major* Hahn's. I pulled up toward the south. At an altitude of about 2000 m, two machines approached me and I identified them as Lagg-5's. I turned immediately to the Lagg-5's going down steeply. I saw that they followed an Me 109. I shot interference fire with all weapons, after which the Lagg-5's abandoned the attack and pulled up to the south. The attacked Me 109 flew in low-level flight toward the northwest in the direction of our own territory. I could not see signs of shooting damage at the Me 109. While I followed the two Lagg-5's, I heard during the now ensuing dogfight about 2 minutes later in the radio: "*Achtung! Achtung! Vater* ("Father" was Assi Hahn's radio identification name), has to make an emergency landing. - "*Achtung! Achtung! Vater* must make an emergency landing!" It was not possible to follow the *Major* because I was involved in another battle."

Therefore, it is quite certain that your husband received some hits in his machine during this aerial battle, that he had to make an emergency landing in enemy territory and may have become a prisoner of the Russians. I had the area in question searched for the emergency-landed machine during the whole afternoon by planes of the *Geschwader*, but nothing was found. After the last interrogations of Russian prisoners of war, we have been assured again and again that German flyers are transported to a prisoner of war camp in the area of Moscow. I have the justified hope that your husband, provided the emergency landing went smoothly, will return to you in good health after the end of the war.

You are aware that I have known your husband from the time prior to Werneuchen' and that is why I requested him for my *Geschwader*. I can assure, dear esteemed Lady, that his loss has deeply affected not only me but all members of the *Geschwader* and particularly his *Gruppe*. It was only the day before yesterday that he attended the celebration of the 4000th air victory of the *Geschwader* with *Leutnant* Stotz, his constant companion, at the command post with me. With his humorous and positive ways, he always made all of us happy. He was not only the commander of his group but also a good father to his men. This is the name his men called him and also his call name in the air. He gained the trust of his superiors and his charges in the shortest of time. Because of his superior pilot expertise and his personal willingness he stimulated the pilots in his *Gruppe* again and again and led them to outstanding performances. The gap caused by his absence will be hard to close. We all are left with the hope that he will return after the eastern front campaign in good health from the being a prisoner of war of the Russians. I will immediately inform you when I hear anything about him.

Cordial greetings,
yours,

Hannes Trautloft

Next page; **Major Hannes Trautloft Geschwaderkommodore** *of JG 54 awarded the Knight's Cross on 27 July 1941. In his Messerschmitt Bf 109 F-2.*

And a few weeks later:

J.G. 54   Command Post, 8 March 1943
KOMMODORE

Dear Madame,

I can give you the joyful news that your husband is alive and uninjured in Russian war captivity. This news was confirmed by several Russian prisoners and downed pilots. According to several interrogations on airfields close to the front, your husband was transported to the rear areas in the direction of Moscow. Purportedly, all German pilots are held there in a large POW camp. There is no additional news. We hope together with you, dear Madame, that your husband will return in good health after the victorious conclusion of the Eastern Campaign.

Cordially yours,
Hannes Trautloft

The following letter was written to Assi's Wife by Dr. Sieh, who also recounted the last flight of Assi Hahn:

28 February, 43

Dear esteemed Lady,

It is very hard for me to write to you because I unfortunately have to convey to you very painful news. Your husband, our *Kommandeur*, our Father, or Assi, as he was always called, did not return a week ago today from an enemy mission. I am absolutely convinced that he landed safely but unfortunately behind enemy lines. I am convinced that he is a prisoner of war in good health and that he will return to you after the end of the war. I am saying this as a small consolation in your great sadness. The long time before the end of the war will certainly be agony for you, but you can be sure with me that he will return after the war.

Let me report to you in detail all I experienced here at the command post. On Saturday, we had a good weather prognosis for the next day, and we all went to bed at 20:30 hours to be fresh for the next day. Your husband came to the command post at about 0700, and because there was some activity at the front, your husband started with 6 machines at 08:55 hours. His battle comrade Stotz flew with your husband as always. When the machines returned, the two first machines wiggled their wings, and we were happy because it was clear to us that the *Kommandeur* and Stotz again had victories. I did not trust my ears when I heard that the *Kommandeur* did not land. I ordered Stotz to come to me and interrogated him in detail. Stotz was absolutely sure that the *Kommandeur* made an emergency landing in our own territory. We were all relieved. Nonetheless, we called all posts requesting a search for the *Kommandeur*.

After several hours we received a report from the forward infantry post by a pilot communications officer that the infantry saw a German fighter pilot land behind the Russian line. This news hit us like a bomb. *Leutnant* Stotz started with his machines immediately to search for the machine from the air in the indicated area. Despite a search of several hours, they could not find anything. In the evening, several confirmed reports from different posts asserted that a German fighter pilot landed further to the east behind the enemy lines. The weather was so bad on the following day that we could not fly. We could not form a raiding party with the purpose of getting prisoners in the area to find out something from them because the Russians were too strong at that location and such a raid would have cost us too many losses. In the course of time it was confirmed that your husband landed there. What had happened in the air? The 6 machines were involved in air combat with Russian fighters. The *Kommandeur* and *Leutnant* Stotz each shot down a fighter.

This victory was your husband's 108th and, at the same time, the 1500th of the group. What a joy it would have been for your husband of he had had the 1500th victory of the group as its *Kommandeur*. In the course of this aerial battle, *Leutnant* Stotz lost sight of your husband. Unfortunately, the radio in the machine was not clear, so that there was no contact with the *Kommandeur*. After that, your husband attacked another enemy fighter and followed him down. During this pursuit, 2 enemy fighters followed your husband's machine and attacked him. Your husband then radioed "Attention, Father is being taught a lesson." After that, a *Feldwebel* chased the fighters away with several salvos, then pulled up. Shortly after this, the *Kommandeur* radioed: "Attention, Father must make an emergency landing" and flew at low altitude in the direction of our own lines.

Unfortunately, Stotz did not see all of this otherwise he would have looked for your husband immediately. All other machines were now involved on other aerial combats so that nobody could watch for your husband. From all we know we can conclude that your husband landed smoothly. I believe that he thought he was making the emergency landing on our own territory and must have been very surprised when the Russians came. In the area where he made the emergency landing, very strong Russian forces were concentrated at that time, so that fleeing was not possible.

In any case, dear esteemed Lady, please be of good hope that you will see your husband again after the war. This will be hard for your husband because he always was worried about being a prisoner of war; we spoke of this during the preceding evening.

Your husband's personal effects have been packed under my supervision, and we will send them to you sometime.

Now, my dear esteemed Lady, do not be too sad and desperate. You have the justified hope that you will get your husband back after the end of the war. He will surely be in good health because he will certainly survive the hard times thanks to his physical condition and vitality.

Take my deeply felt sympathy for the heavy blow fate has dealt you.
Cordially,

Dr. Sieh

Interrogation of a Russian pilot prisoner by the German authorities provides information about Assi Hahn in captivity:

Prisoner Interrogation No. 208 dated 12 April 1943, of Krjutschkow, Leonid Semjonowitsch, born 19 June 1920 in Wojeikowo, District Rjasan. Sub Leutnant, pilot and acting escadrille leader of the 1st Escadrille of the 674th independent mixed army pilot regiment (674th ossap). Under the command of the 1st Shock Army.

Shot down on 2 March 43 near Staraja Russia by an Me 109.

German Prisoners of War.
The prisoner saw *Major* Hans Hahn uninjured on the airfield Saborowje. Hahn had to make an emergency landing at the street of Nowaha Derewnja to Marewo near Ustmwewo (c. 20 km west of Molwotizy), after he himself had shot down 3 Russians, among them one "Hero of the Soviet Union." According to the statements by the prisoner's comrades, *Major* Hahn is said to be a wearer of the *Ritterkreuz* and of five other medals; he is said to have had 108 victories. He was sitting in the dining room in Saborowje and was moved to Wypolsowo where he was detained in his own room three days ago, according to statements by U-2 pilots who fly often to this destination. He was said to have practiced boxing with Russian pilots. He is said to be well.

F. d. R. d. A.
//signature//
Major

Chapter 8 Notes:

1. Spelled as Demiansk in book written by Assi Hahn, "I Speak the Truth".
2. Actually La-5s, many wartime Germany reports incorrectly identified the Lavochkin La-5 as "Lagg-5s" a non-existent aircraft.
3. Fighter Pilot's School they both attended.

Chapter Nine
Homecoming and Post War

𝔍inally, after seven long, grueling years in Soviet captivity, Assi Hahn was released and returned to Germany by train a short time before Christmas 1950. Upon his arrival he was warmly greeted by a gathering of friends that included his young son, missing was his wife who had given up hope on Assi's return, replacing him with a new man in her life.

Starting over in post-war Germany was not easy but Assi excelled at adversity. Some friends took him into their home where he lived in a kind of tower where he wrote his controversial book "I Speak the Truth". Obtaining employment at the International Corporation of Bayer Leverkusen, he was soon discovered by a superior who knew his reputation as a strong leader. As a result, Assi was promoted to a position of International trade dealing with France and England. A career change came later when he became a director at the Wano Schwarzpulver company at Kunigunde located near Goslar, Germany, that manufactured black powder. Here he worked until his retirement in 1977.

Upon learning of his good friend Erich Hartmann's release, mid October 1955, after being held ten years by the Russians, Assi was at the Friedland train station in Germany to welcome Erich back home. The two had formed a strong bond built around mutual respect for surviving the unspeakable ordeal with their honor intact. Assi had planned a grand celebration, but Erich's brother Alfred, arrived to drive him directly to his anxiously waiting wife Usch.

Assi would soon meet a person that would change his life forever – Gisela von Vietinghoff. It was almost love at first sight as the initial spark grew into a flame and eventually they were united in marriage on 22 January 1971. Kai, Gisela's youngest of her three sons from a previous marriage, moved into the Hahn household where Assi gave him positive guidance through the difficult times of youth for which Kai is extremely grateful to this day. After Assi's retirement in 1977 the Hahns relocated to a villa in southern France

where he was able to seriously pursue another one of his passions: cactus gardening.

Life was full and eventful as Assi's popularity never waned even after his retirement. Many of their friends, including former Luftwaffe personalities, former Wehrmacht officers and even an ex-torpedo boat captain frequented their home. Gisela's other two boys Olaf and Andreas would also spend their holidays and free time at the Hahn's French villa.

Gisela and Assi's life together was filled with years of golden and magical times until a foe that even Assi could not defeat took his life – cancer. Assi Hahn died from this dreaded disease on 18 December 1982 in München Germany at the age of 68.

Assi Hahn was laid to rest in the cemetery behind a quaint Catholic church in St. Tirol Austria.

"Now his eventful and partially dramatic life has come to an end. We are grateful and happy that fate has bestowed on us his acquaintance and friendship." - **Julius Meimberg**, Assi's Life-long friend who spoke at the memorial services.

Biographical Notes

- ✠ Born 14 April 1914 in Gotha, Germany

- ✠ Uniform grade school from Easter 1921 to Easter 1925

- ✠ Academic high school in Gotha from April 1925 to March 1934

- ✠ Qualified for University studies, Easter 1934

- ✠ Entered the Infantry Regiment Nr. 14 on 1 April 1934 as officer candidate

- ✠ *Gefreiter* in May 1934; *Unteroffizier* 1 December 1934

- ✠ Attended the *Kriegsschule* (War College) in München from Jan. 1935 to Oct. 1935

- ✠ Promoted to *Oberfähnrich* on 1 October 1935

- ✠ Changed to the *Luftwaffe* in November 1935; transferred to pilot school in Celle

- ✠ Promoted to *Leutnant* on 1 April 1936

- ✠ After completing training, transferred to the *Jagdgeschwader* JG 134 *"Horst Wessel"* in Werl on 15 April 1936

- ✠ Transferred on 1 November 1937 as Company Leader in the newly-founded *Jagdfliegerschule* at Werneuchen to be a flight instructor

- ✠ *Stab* I./JG 3 *"Udet"* Merseburg, 1939

- ✠ Transferred to JG 2 *"Richthofen"*, October 1939

- ✠ 15 December 1939 promoted to *Staffelkapitän* of 4./JG 2

- ✠ Awarded the E.K. II , *Eiserne Kreuz* (Iron Cross) on 29 May 1940 and E.K. I in early July, 1940

- ✠ Awarded the *Ritterkreuz* (Knight's Cross) 24 September 1940 after his 20th air victory

- ✠ Promoted to *Hauptmann* and *Gruppenkommandeur* of III. *Gruppe Jagdgeschwader "Richthofen"* 29 October 1940

- ✠ Awarded *Frontflug-Spange* in Gold (combat clasp) 26 April 1941

- ✠ Awarded *Eichenlaubs zum Ritterkreuz* (Oak Leaves to the Knight's Cross) on 14 August 1941 after his 42nd air victory

- ✠ Awarded the *Deutches Kreuz* (German Cross) 16 July 1942

- ✠ Transferred to II./JG 54 *"Grünherz"* (Green Hearts), Russia, 1 November 1942

- ✠ Promoted to *Major* 1 January 1943

- ✠ Downed behind Russian lines, 21 February 1943, prisoner for seven years; Released from Russian captivity in 1950

- ✠ 22 January 1971 married Gisela von Vietinghoff

- ✠ Retired from Wano Black Powder company 1977

- ✠ 18 December 1982, at the age of 68, passed away as a result of cancer

Portrait Gallery

Knight's Cross now with Oak leaves, is apparent.
Oak Leaves were awarded to Assi on 14 August 1941.

Hptm. Hahn, taken at St. Pol, France.

Hptm. Hahn with a pet bird. Assi is holding his Abschußstock, (victory stick) that was presented to him by fellow pilots.

Portrait photo postcard of Hptm. Assi Hahn with his Knight's Cross with Oak Leaves.

*Oblt. Hahn with
Knight's Cross*

*Left; Oblt. Hahn, notable is the
Jagdgeschwader "Richthofen" cuff title
on his right sleeve.*

*Assi Hahn wearing a **Schwimmweste**, seated in one of his aircraft. Note the padded armored headrest, no overhead armor in
the canopy. Good view of the **Revi C 12/D** gun sight.*

Assi Hahn travel pass document, post war.

Assi Hahn's business card, post war, states "Ready any time for new deals"

Chapter Ten

The Machines

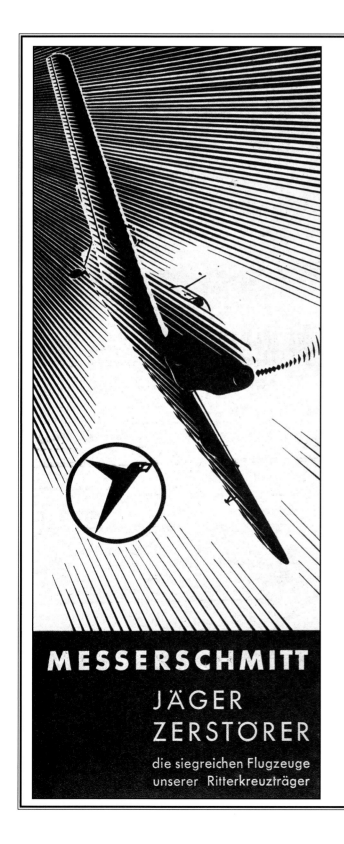

TECHNICAL DATA

Messerschmitt Bf 109 E-3 and Bf 109 E-4

The Messerschmitt **Bf 109 E-3** began its service life in Autumn 1938, it was faster and more heavily armed than the **Bf 109 E-1**.

Power Plant:	DB601 Aa 1150 hp
Fuel Requirements:	87 octane
Armament:	2 MG 17 7.92 mm machine guns mounted over the engine (staggered); 1000 rounds per gun. 2 MG FF Oerlikon 20 mm cannons mounted in the wing; 60 rounds per gun. A proposed MG FF Oerlikon 20 mm cannon engine mounted firing through propeller hub was never utilized.
Wheel and tire size:	Main; 650 mm X 150 mm. Tail wheel; 290 mm X 110 mm.
Dimensions:	Wingspan 9870 mm, 32' 4 ½"; Length 8640 mm, 28' 4 ½"

The Messerschmitt **Bf 109 E-4** essentially was the same aircraft as the **Bf 109 E-3**. According to Messerschmitt documents, the only difference between the E-3 and the E-4 was the introduction of the MG-FF/M cannons with a projectile having a faster muzzle velocity and the addition of armor for the E-4. Both features were later retrofitted to many E-1s and E-3s. The spinners on some production E-4s were capped. A later variation fitted with the DB 601 N engine of 1175 hp was designated Bf 109 E-4/N. Most production E-4s were equipped with the square style canopy. Without knowing the Werknummer it is almost impossible to determine individual aircraft's identity between these two versions.

Power Plant:	DB601 Aa 1150 hp
Fuel Requirements:	87 octane
Armament:	2 MG 17 7.92 mm machine guns mounted over the engine (staggered); 1000 rounds per gun. 2 MG FF/M Oerlikon 20 mm cannons mounted in the wing; 60 rounds per gun.
Wheel and tire size:	Main; 650 mm X 150 mm. Tail wheel; 290 mm X 110 mm.
Dimensions:	Wingspan 9870 mm, 32' 4 ½"; Length 8640 mm, 28' 4 ½"

Color Reference Chart

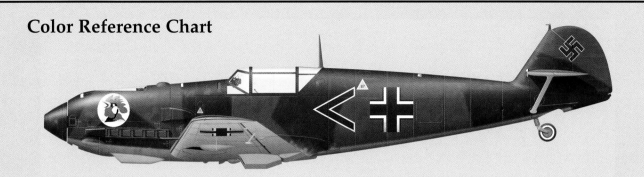

Assi Hahn   Aircraft No. 1   Bf 109 E-3   "Chevron"

W. Nr. Unknown   Stab I./JG 3   September 1939   Merseburg, Germany

For a short while, Assi Hahn was on the Stab of I./JG 3 *"Udet"* stationed at Merseburg, Germany before he was assigned to JG 2 *"Richthofen"* in October 1939.

Notable features of this machine include:
- ✠ No cockpit head armor
- ✠ RLM 65 Light Blue machine gun troughs
- ✠ White wall tire on tail wheel

COLORS

UNDERSURFACES   RLM 65 Light Blue

UPPERSURFACES   RLM 71 Dark Green/RLM 70 Black-Green, RLM 65 gun troughs

SPINNER & PROP BLADES   RLM 70 Black-Green

STAB MARKINGS   Single Black Chevron with White outline on both sides of fuselage

PERSONAL EMBLEM   Large early style Rooster Head, (Hahn in German means Rooster) on both sides of engine cowling

NATIONAL MARKINGS

FUSELAGE   B2 style 660 mm Black/White crosses with thin Black outline
                             H2 Black/White *Hakenkreuz* with thin Black outline

WINGS   Upper and Lower: B2 style 660 mm Black/White crosses with thin Black outline

STENCILLING - Factory Standard

Color Reference Chart

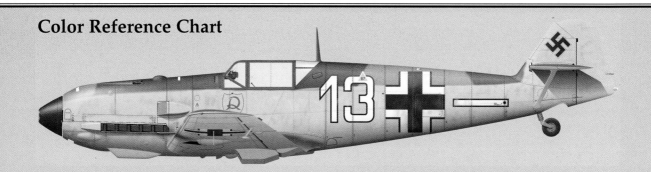

Assi Hahn Aircraft No. 2   Bf 109 E-3   "White 13"

| W. Nr. Unknown | 4./JG 2 | Spring 1940 | Northern, Germany |

This machine was flown by Assi Hahn during the Spring of 1940.

Notable features of this machine include:

✠   Square canopy with no head armor; E-3s and E-4s could be fitted with either the rounded canopy and the square canopy, however the square canopy became standard equipment on the E-4s.

✠   The JG 2 *"Richthofen"* shield emblem appears on this aircraft in late Spring, 1940.

COLORS

UNDERSURFACES	RLM 65 Light Blue extending up to the fuselage, even with the canopy
UPPERSURFACES	RLM 02 Gray / RLM 71 Dark Green
SPINNER & PROP BLADES	RLM 70 Black-Green
TACTICAL MARKINGS	Large White 13 with Black outline and matching II. *Gruppe* bar behind fuselage crosses
UNIT EMBLEM	JG 2 *"Richthofen"* Red "R" in shield with no background color, on both sides under wind screen

NATIONAL MARKINGS

FUSELAGE	B2 style 900 mm Black/White crosses with thin Black outline H2 Black/White *Hakenkreuz* with thin Black outline
WINGS	Upper: B2 style 1000 mm Black/White with thin Black outline Lower: B2 style 900 mm Black/White crosses with thin Black outline (Some sources specify 950 mm, others 900 mm)

STENCILLING - Factory Standard

Color Reference Chart

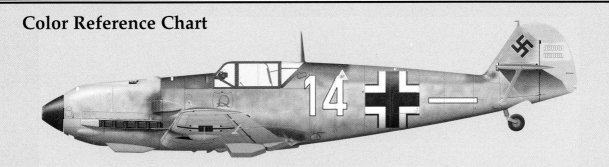

Assi Hahn   Aircraft No. 3   Bf 109 E-4   "White 14"

W. Nr. Unknown	4./JG 2	Summer 1940	France

This Bf 109 E-4 was flown by Assi Hahn during the Battle of Britain. His 20 victories are recorded on its rudder for which we received the Knight's Cross on 24 September 1940. This is the machine Hahn attempted to land in Carentan, France in the Bog Ghost incident. It flipped over breaking in half. 18 October 1940

Notable features of this machine include:
✠ Square canopy with pilot's armored head rest and overhead armor

COLORS

UNDERSURFACES   RLM 65 Light Blue

UPPERSURFACES   RLM 71 Dark Green/RLM 02 Gray, heavy mottling on sides of fuselage with RLM 02 Gray. RLM 04 Yellow cowling stained and weathered, RLM 04 Rudder except for area of Light Blue behind victory bars.

SPINNER & PROP BLADES   RLM 70 Black-Green (Spinner possibly RLM 04 Yellow)

TACTICAL MARKINGS   White 14 with then Black outline and matching II. *Gruppe* bar

UNIT EMBLEM   JG 2 *"Richthofen"* Red "R" in shield with no background color on both sides under wind screen

NATIONAL MARKINGS

FUSELAGE   B2 style 900 mm Black/White crosses with thin Black outline
                           H2 Black/White *Hakenkreuz* with thin Black outline

WINGS   Upper: B2 style 1000 mm Black/White crosses with thin Black outline
                           Lower: B2 style 900 mm Black/White crosses with thin Black outline
                            (Some sources specify 950 mm, others 900 mm)

STENCILLING
Factory Standard, 20 White victory bars with thin Black outline on rudder, both sides.

Color Reference Chart

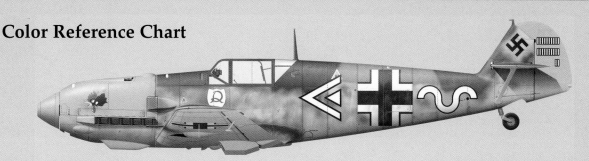

Assi Hahn   Aircraft No. 4   Bf 109 E-4   Chevron with Triangle

W. Nr. Unknown   III./JG 2   Fall 1940   Le Havre, France

Assi Hahn was promoted to Gruppenkommandeur of III./JG 2 on 29 October 1940. This colorful E-4 was his new aircraft with 22 victory bars on the rudder dating it November 1940.
Notable features of this machine include:
- ✵ Square canopy with pilot's armored head rest and overhead armor

COLORS

UNDERSURFACES	RLM 65 Light Blue
UPPERSURFACES	RLM 71 Dark Green/RLM 02 Gray, heavy mottling on sides of fuselage with RLM 02 Gray. RLM 04 Yellow cowling, spinner and rudder
PROP BLADES	RLM 70 Black-Green
STAB MARKINGS	White *Kommandeur* Chevron and triangle with thin Black outline with matching III. *Gruppe Welle* (wave) behind the fuselage crosses.
UNIT EMBLEM	JG 2 *"Richthofen"* Red "R" on White shield on both sides under wind screen
PERSONAL EMBLEM	A new streamlined rooster head on both sides of engine cowling adopted and used on III. *Gruppe* aircraft, provisional on this machine.

NATIONAL MARKINGS

FUSELAGE	B2 style 900 mm Black/White crosses with thin Black outline H2 Black/White *Hakenkreuz* with thin Black outline
WINGS	Upper: B2 style 1000 mm Black/White crosses with thin Black outline Lower: B2 style 900 mm Black/White crosses with thin Black outline (Some sources specify 950 mm, others 900 mm)

STENCILLING

Factory Standard, 22 White victory bars with thin Black outline on rudder, both sides.

Technical Data

Messerschmitt Bf 109 F

To improve the squarish looking Bf 109 series, the Messerschmitt design team developed the new stream-lined F type. External changes included a more aerodynamic engine cowling, rounded spinner and wing tips, an improved supercharger air intake, re-designed flap system, flatter wing radiators for the glycol coolant, and the horizontal tail braces were eliminated. Tail wheel semi-retractable. Many pilots preferred the F type of Bf 109 over all others as it was light, fast and maneuverable.

	Bf 109 F-2	**Bf 109 F-4**
Power Plant:	DB601 N 1175 hp	DB 601 E 1350 hp
Fuel Requirements:	C3 96 octane	87 octane
Propeller:	VDM 9-11207 A (3 m dia.)	VDM 9-12010 A (3 m dia.)
Armament:	1 MG 151/15 mm Engine mounted cannon; 200 rounds 2 MG 17 7.92 mm machine guns mounted over the engine (staggered); 500 rounds per gun	1 MG 151/20 mm Engine mounted cannon; 150 rounds 2 MG 17 7.92 mm machine guns mounted over the engine (staggered); 500 rounds per gun
Wheel and tire size:	Main; 650 mm X 150 mm Tail wheel; 290 mm X 110 mm	Main; 650 mm X 150 mm Tail wheel; 290 mm X 110 mm
Dimensions:	Wingspan 9924 mm; 32' 6 ½" Length 8940 mm; 29' 7 1/8"	Wingspan 9924 mm; 32' 6 ½" Length 8940 mm; 29' 7 1/8"

Color Reference Chart

Assi Hahn Aircraft No. 5   Bf 109 F-2   "Chevron with Triangle"

W. Nr. 5749   III./JG 2   Mid July 1941   St. Pol, France

First known F series aircraft flown by Assi Hahn. This F-2 was photographed after his 31st victory on 10 July 1941. This photo was published in Karl Ries Jr.'s classic book Dora Kurfürst und Rote 13 in 1964. The film type used in taking this photo caused the Yellow cowling to turn dark and initially was interpreted as Red, sparking controversy among enthusiasts. By comparing the color of the Rooster's comb, which appears to be almost Black in the photo, but is known to be Red, the engine cowling appears lighter or Yellow. This photo does show the under cowling a slightly lighter value than the upper cowling. This was caused by Yellow painted over Light Blue of the under cowling and Yellow painted over the Grays of the upper cowling, resulting in a slightly darker value.

Notable features of this machine include:

✠ Canopy equipped with pilot's armored heard rest and overhead armor

COLORS

UNDERSURFACES	RLM 76 Light Blue
UPPERSURFACES	RLM 75 Gray-Violet/RLM 74 Gray-Green. RLM 04 Yellow cowling and rudder. Black area around exhaust and wing root.
SPINNER / PROP BLADES	White with RLM 70 Black-Green section. RLM 70 Black-Green section.
STAB MARKINGS	White *Kommandeur* Chevron and triangle with thin Black outline with matching vertical III. *Gruppe* bar behind the fuselage crosses, provisional, not visible in photo. Hahn changed this standard vertical bar to a band encircling the rear fuselage.
UNIT EMBLEM	JG 2 *"Richthofen"* Red "R" on White shield on both sides under wind screen
PERSONAL EMBLEM	Streamlined rooster head on both sides of engine cowling adopted and used on III. *Gruppe* aircraft

NATIONAL MARKINGS

FUSELAGE	B2 style 900 mm Black/White crosses with thin Black outline H2a Black/White *Hakenkreuz*
WINGS	Upper: B2 style 1000 mm Black/White crosses with thin Black outline Lower: B2 style 900 mm Black/White crosses with thin Black outline (Some sources specify 950 mm, others 900 mm)

STENCILLING

Factory Standard, 31 Black victory bars on rudder, both sides.

Color Reference Chart

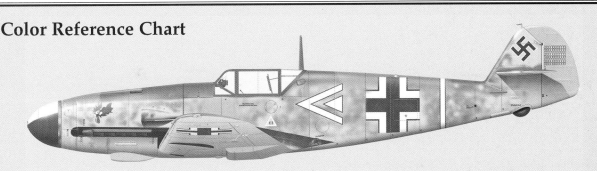

Assi Hahn Aircraft No. 6   Bf 109 F-2   "Chevron with Triangle"

W. Nr. 5749?   III./JG 2   Mid-July 1941   St. Pol, France

This F-2 appears to be Hahn's earlier aircraft *Werknummer* 5749 but now partially repainted. The Yellow cowling is now reduced to the undercowling only, the Hahn style III. *Gruppe* fuselage band is clearly in place and note how the area around this band appears to be freshly painted. A new longer and leaner *Stab* chevron is in place and the JG 2 shield is now painted out for security reasons. (JG 26 removed their *Schlageter* emblem at this time as well.) The 31 victory bars on the rudder are now more elaborate, displaying English or French roundels within each bar. The Black area around the exhaust is now rounded at the front. After examining all of these details, it could be a different machine as the *Werknummer* is not visible in the photos. The pilot's overhead armor has been removed.

COLORS

UNDERSURFACES	RLM 76 Light Blue
UPPERSURFACES	RLM 75 Gray-Violet/RLM 74 Gray-Green. RLM 04 Yellow cowling and rudder. Black area around exhaust and wing root.
SPINNER/ PROP BLADES	White with RLM 70 Black-Green section. RLM 70 Black-Green section.
STAB MARKINGS	White *Kommandeur* Chevron and triangle with thin Black outline, longer and leaner than previously; matching III. *Gruppe* band encircling rear fuselage.
UNIT EMBLEM	JG 2 *"Richthofen"* emblem has now been painted out.
PERSONAL EMBLEM	Streamlined rooster head on both sides of engine cowling adopted and used on III. *Gruppe* aircraft

NATIONAL MARKINGS

FUSELAGE	B2 style 900 mm Black/White crosses with thin Black outline H2a Black/White *Hakenkreuz*
WINGS	Upper: B2 style 1000 mm Black/White crosses with thin Black outline Lower: B2 style 900 mm Black/White crosses with thin Black outline (Some sources specify 950 mm, others 900 mm)

STENCILLING

Factory Standard. The 31 Black victory bars on both sides of the rudder, are now White with thin Black outline, the Red French roundels being recorded as the 4th, 5th and 6th victory claims, but were corrected to 3rd, 4th and 5th on the later Fw 190 rudder, W. Nr. 223.

Color Reference Chart

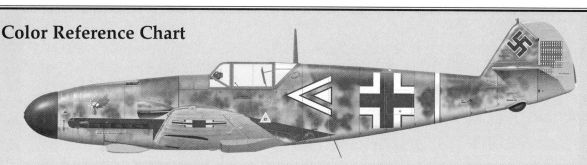

Assi Hahn   Aircraft No. 7   Bf 109 F-4   "Chevron with Triangle"
W. Nr. 7183   III./JG 2   27 September 1941   St. Pol, France

This F-4 is well documented photographically both by official and personal sources. After Hahn had been awarded the Oak Leaves to his Knight's Cross on 14 August 1941, he achieved celebrity status and was constantly in the public eye. Compare the position of the rooster head, where the peak of the Black wing root is positioned on the side of the fuselage, and the overall camouflage pattern of this aircraft to other similarly painted III. *Gruppe* aircraft to properly identify Assi Hahn's machine. A reliable method to help identify an F-4 from an F-2 is the presence of the 87 octane triangle on the fuselage under the fuel access panel. The F-2 octane stencil indicates C3 fuel requirement, 96 octane.

Notable features of this machine include:
- Canopy equipped with pilot's armored heard rest without overhead armor
- Clean and well-maintained condition as demanded by Assi Hahn
- FuG 25 a antenna intact

COLORS

UNDERSURFACES   RLM 76 Light Blue

UPPERSURFACES   RLM 75 Gray-Violet/RLM 74 Gray-Green, heavily mottled.
                         RLM 04 Yellow under cowling and rudder. Area behind victory bars is Gray.
                         Black area around exhaust and wing root.

SPINNER & PROP BLADES   RLM 70 Black-Green

STAB MARKINGS   White *Kommandeur* Chevron and triangle with thin Black outline and matching
                         III. *Gruppe* band encircling rear fuselage.

PERSONAL EMBLEM   Streamlined rooster head on both sides of engine cowling adopted and used on
                         III. *Gruppe* aircraft

NATIONAL MARKINGS

FUSELAGE   B2 style 900 mm Black/White crosses with thin Black outline
                         H2a Black/White *Hakenkreuz*

WINGS   Upper: B2 style 1000 mm Black/White crosses with thin Black outline
                         Lower: B2 style 900 mm Black/White crosses with thin Black outline
                         (Some sources specify 950 mm, others 900 mm)

STENCILLING

Factory Standard, note 87 octane fuel triangle below cockpit area helped identify this as an F-4 sub-type. 46 White with thin Black outline victory bars over Gray area of Yellow rudder, both sides.

Color Reference Chart

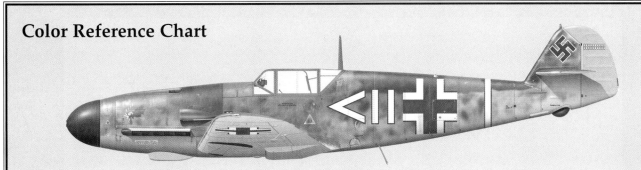

Pilot: Oblt. Puchinger	**Bf 109 F-4**	**"Chevron Double Bar"**
W. Nr. unknown	III./JG 2 Summer 1941	St. Pol, France

Normally the *Stab* chevron with two vertical bars was the identification marking for the *Geschwaderstab Major* (Chief of Staff), but Assi Hahn had a chief of Staff on his *Gruppenstab*. He was Oblt. Josef Puchinger and this was his aircraft.

Notable features of this machine include:
- ✠ Canopy with pilot's armored head rest and overhead armor
- ✠ FuG 25 a antenna intact

COLORS

UNDERSURFACES	RLM 76 Light Blue
UPPERSURFACES	RLM 75 Gray-Violet/ RLM 74 Gray-Green, heavy mottling on fuselage. RLM 04 Yellow undercowling and rudder.
SPINNER & PROP BLADES	RLM 70 Black-Green
STAB MARKINGS	White chevron plus two vertical bars with thin Black outline, matching III. *Gruppe* band encircling rear fuselage
UNIT EMBLEM	Streamlined rooster head on both sides of engine cowling adopted and used on III. *Gruppe* aircraft
NATIONAL MARKINGS	
FUSELAGE	B2 style 900 mm Black/White crosses with thin Black outline; note cross is slightly forward of being centered between panel lines. H2a Black/White *Hakenkreuz*
WINGS	Upper: B2 style 1000 mm Black/White crosses with thin Black outline Lower: B2 style 900 mm Black/White crosses with thin Black outline (Some sources specify 950 mm, others 900 mm)

STENCILLING - Factory Standard

TECHNICAL DATA

Focke-Wulf Fw 190 A-2 and Fw 190 A-3

Once the engine cooling and other problems were worked out, the pilots' confidence grew and the Focke-Wulf 190 became a superior new fighter. The A-2 and A-3 sub-types are externally the same aircraft. Internally the A-3 was updated with the more powerful BMW 801 D-2 engine putting out 1700 hp. Many A-3 aircraft also had their outboard wing mounted MG FF 20 mm cannons deleted.

	Fw 190 A-2	**Fw 190 A-3**
Power Plant:	BMW C-2 1600 hp 12 bladed cooling fan	BMW D-2 1700 hp 12 bladed cooling fan
Fuel Requirements:	C3 96 octane	C3 96 octane
Propeller:	Metal VDM 9-12067 3.3 m diameter	Metal VDM 9-12067 3.3 m diameter
Armament:	2 MG 17 7.92 mm machine guns mounted over the engine 1000 rounds per gun 2 MG 151 20 mm cannons mounted inboard wing 200 rounds per gun 2 MG FF Oerlikon 20 mm cannons outboard wing position 55 rounds per gun	2 MG 17 7.92 mm machine guns mounted over the engine 1000 rounds per gun 2 MG 151 20 mm cannons mounted inboard wing 200 rounds per gun 2 MG FF Oerlikon 20 mm cannons outboard wing position 55 rounds per gun, deleted on many A-3s
Wheel and tire size:	Main; 700 mm X 175 mm Tail wheel; 380 mm X 150 mm	Main; 700 mm X 175 mm Tail Wheel; 380 mm X 150 mm
Dimensions:	Wingspan 10500 mm, 34' 5 ½" Length 8850 mm, 28' 10 ½"	Wingspan 10500 mm, 34' 5 ½" Length 8850 mm, 28' 10 ½"

Color Reference Chart

Assi Hahn Aircraft No. 8   Fw 190 A-2   White Chevron with Triangle

W. Nr. 223   III./JG 2   May 1942   Beaumont-le-Roger, France

This aircraft was built by the main factory at Bremen, Germany. The 61 victories recorded on the Yellow rudder indicate the date to be after 6 May 1942. Also, the French victories have now been corrected to numbers 3, 4 and 5. Compare this to Hahn's earlier Bf 109 F-4 rudder.

Notable features of this machine include:

- The overall pristine condition of this aircraft is noteworthy as Hahn was demanding of his ground crew to keep his aircraft well maintained.
- FuG 25a antenna mast intact
- Typical small rectangular bump on rear of gun cowling

COLORS

UNDERSURFACES   RLM 76 Light Blue or RLM 65 Light Blue

UPPERSURFACES   Some sources indicate these early Fw 190s inherited the Bf 109 E camouflage color combination of RLM 02 Gray/RLM 71 Dark Green. Other sources claim the combination of Grays to be RLM 75 Gray-Violet/ 74 Gray-Green. (see technical report on A-3 W. Nr. 5 313). Illustrated herein is RLM 75 Gray-Violet/RLM 74 Gray-Green combination as choice. RLM 04 Yellow rudder and undercowling.

SPINNER & PROP BLADES   RLM 70 Black-Green

STAB MARKINGS   White *Kommandeur* Chevron and triangle with thin Black outline; matching III. *Gruppe* band encircling rear fuselage.

PERSONAL EMBLEM   Streamlined rooster head on both sides of engine cowling adopted and used on III. *Gruppe* aircraft

NATIONAL MARKINGS

FUSELAGE   B2 style 800 mm Black/White crosses with thin Black outline
                      H2 Black/White *Hakenkreuz* with thin Black outline

WINGS   Upper: B2 style 910 mm Black/White crosses with thin Black outline
                      Lower: B2 style 900 mm Black/White crosses with thin Black outline

STENCILLING

Factory standard. W. Nr. 223 on both sides of fin.

Color Reference Chart

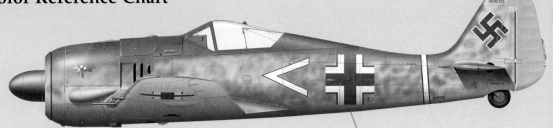

Assi Hahn Aircraft No. 9   Fw 190 A-3   White Chevron

| W. Nr. 5 313 | III./JG 2 | May/June 1942 | Cherbourg, France |

Built by Arado Warnemünde, Germany, Assi Hahn occasionally flew this *Stab* machine. This was the famous aircraft inadvertently delivered to the RAF on 23 June 1942 by Oblt. Armin Faber, *Stab* officer of III. JG 2. After an air battle with Spitfires, Faber became disoriented and mistakenly landed at Pembrey at 20:35 hours. This was the first Fw 190 to be captured and thoroughly tested by various British air establishments who reported their findings. Two of which are quoted here:

1. Aircraft Engineering, March 1943 issue, describes the camouflage as "the normal (German) fighter camouflage was used on this aeroplane. That is, the top and sides were mottled Blue-Gray and the undersurface pale Blue. The rudder was painted Yellow." No mention of the Yellow undercowling, or of any Green, (RLM 71 Dark Green) or Gray (RLM 02 Gray-Green).
2. RAF intelligence report describes the camouflage as Dark Green, Light Olive Green and Pale Blue with Yellow nose and rudder.

Notable features of this machine include:
   ✠   FuG 25 a antenna mast intact
   ✠   Typical small rectangular bump plus a round distinctive bump on rear of gun cowling.

COLORS

UNDERSURFACES	RLM 76 Light Blue, or RLM 65 Light Blue
UPPERSURFACES	RLM 75 Gray-Violet/RLM 74 Gray-Green or RLM 02 Gray/ RLM 71 Dark Green RLM 04 Yellow undercowling and rudder. At the time Faber landed in England, the louvered exhaust panel was painted Black. Color profile illustrated in 74/75/76 combination
SPINNER & PROP BLADES	RLM 70 Black-Green
STAB MARKINGS	White *Kommandeur* Chevron with thin Black outline; matching III. *Gruppe* band encircling rear fuselage.
PERSONAL EMBLEM	Streamlined rooster head on both sides of engine cowling adopted and used on III. *Gruppe* aircraft

NATIONAL MARKINGS

FUSELAGE	B2 style 800 mm Black/White crosses with thin Black outline H2a Black/White *Hakenkreuz*
WINGS	Upper: B2 style 910 mm Black/White crosses with thin Black outline Lower: B2 style 900 mm Black/White crosses with thin Black outline

STENCILLING

Factory Standard. W. Nr. 313 on both sides of fin. Actual *Werknummer* is 5 313, Arado dropped the first number

TECHNICAL DATA

Messerschmitt Bf 109 G-2

The first production Messerschmitt G type to be produced was the G-1 fitted with a pressurized cockpit. Built simultaneously was the G-2 which was non-pressurized eliminating the pressurization system such as the silica gel tablets in the canopy and small air compressor inlet scoop on the port side of the engine cowling above the super charger intake. Carried over from the pressurized cockpit, the vertical bulkhead that sealed the G-1 cockpit was also installed in many of the early G-2s. Additionally, some G-2s lacked the fresh air scoop found on the quarter panel below the side windscreen. The first G-2s were delivered to fighter units beginning in June 1942.

Power Plant:	DB 605 A-1 1475 hp
Fuel Requirements:	87 octane
Propeller:	Metal VDM 9-12087, 3300 mm diameter
Armament:	2 MG 17 7.92 mm machine guns mounted over the engine; 500 rounds per gun 1 MG 151 20 mm cannon mounted in the engine; 150 rounds
Wheel and tire size:	Main: Early; 650 mm X 150 mm Late; 660 mm X 160 mm Required accommodating bumps on the upper wing for the late main wheels Tail Wheel; 350 mm X 135 mm
Dimensions:	Wingspan 9924 mm; 32' 6 ½" Length 8940 mm; 29' 7 1/8"

Color Reference Chart

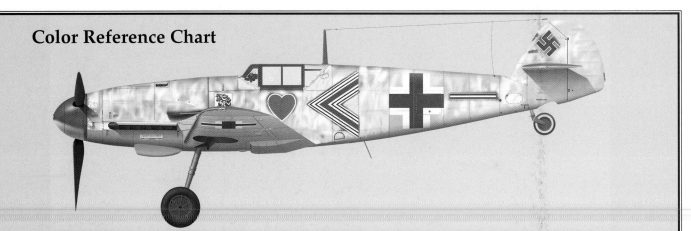

Assi Hahn Aircraft No. 10   Bf 109 G-2   "Chevron with Double Lines"
W. Nr. unknown   II./JG 54   Winter 1942-1943   Rjelbitzy, Russia

This G-2 can be seen in a film of Assi Hahn landing and dismounting at Rjelbitzy airfield in Russia. Once out of the aircraft, he seems to be rather upset about something and is discussing it with his ground crew. Assi then moves to the rear of this machine and talks to his 6. *Staffelkapitän* Hans Beißwenger. This same aircraft was later flown by Hahn's successor to II./JG 54 Hptm. Heinrich Jung.
Notable features of this machine include:

- Vertical bulkhead at rear of canopy
- No fresh air scoops on triangular panel under side windscreen
- FuG 25 a antenna intact
- White side wall tail wheel
- Main landing gear doors removed to eliminate snow impactment

COLORS

UNDERSURFACES   RLM 76 Light Blue

UPPERSURFACES   Possibly RLM 75 Gray-Violet/RLM 74 Gray-Green over sprayed with White for snow cam ouflage, some Gray showing through. Canopy framework mostly RLM 74. (Possibly unusu-al JG 54 camouflage color pattern of Greens and Grays.) RLM 04 Yellow undercowling and underwing tips; Yellow band behind fuselage cross appears to be painted out.

SPINNER/
PROP BLADES   Originally White with RLM 70 Black-Green section, partially over sprayed with White for snow camouflage. Prop Blades, RLM 70 Black-Green

STAB MARKINGS   JG 54 used an unusual style of command chevron on many of their *Stab* aircraft. This one has the most bizarre version of all, a Dark Gray chevron with two White and Black outlines, with the outside border formed by the camouflage color. The II. *Gruppe* bar behind the fuselage cross is made up of two parallel Black lines.

UNIT EMBLEM   Large JG 54 Green Heart under cockpit on both sides. II. *Gruppe* JG 54 emblem Lion of Aspern on forward fuselage, both sides.

NATIONAL MARKINGS

FUSELAGE   B3 style 900 mm Black/White crosses
H2a Black/White *Hakenkreuz*, note overspray with White snow camouflage

WINGS   Upper: B1 style 1000 mm Black/White crosses
Lower: B3 style 900 mm Black/White crosses (Some sources specify 950 mm, others 900)

STENCILLING -   Factory Standard, partially over painted

Color Reference Chart

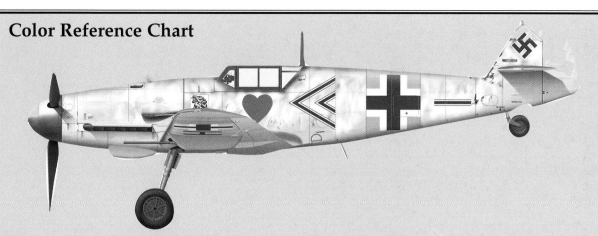

Assi Hahn   Aircraft No. 11   Bf 109 G-2/R6   "Double Chevron"

W. Nr. 13949   II./JG 54   January 1943   Rjelbitzy, Russia

This was the aircraft Major Assi Hahn was flying on his last mission when after engaging Russian La 5s he was forced down and captured.
Notable features of this machine include:

* ✠ Vertical bulkhead at rear of canopy with unusual flat overhead armor plate over pilot's head
* ✠ No fresh air scoops on triangular panel under side windscreen
* ✠ FuG 25 a antenna intact
* ✠ Lower portion of landing gear doors removed to eliminate snow impactment
* ✠ MG 151 20 mm underwing cannon gondolas.
* ✠ Air restrictor panel in oil cooler radiator, see photo

COLORS

UNDERSURFACES   RLM 76 Light Blue

UPPERSURFACES   Possibly RLM 75 Gray-Violet/RLM 74 Gray-Green over sprayed with White for snow cam
ouflage, some Gray showing through. Canopy framework mostly RLM 74. (Possibly unusual JG 54 camouflage color pattern of Greens and Grays.) RLM 04 Yellow undercowling partially overpainted with snow camouflage; Yellow underwing tips; Yellow band behind fuse-
age cross.

SPINNER/   Originally White with RLM 70 Black-Green section, partially over sprayed with White for
PROP BLADES   snow camouflage.   PROP BLADES RLM 70 Black-Green

STAB MARKINGS   Typical Stab chevrons of JG 54, Black with White borders outlined with a thin
Black edge. Matching II. Gruppe bar behind fuselage cross.

UNIT EMBLEM   Large JG 54 Green Heart under cockpit on both sides. II. Gruppe JG 54
emblem Lion of Aspern on forward fuselage, both sides.

NATIONAL MARKINGS

FUSELAGE   B3 style 900 mm Black/White crosses
H2a Black/White Hakenkreuz

WINGS   Upper: B1 style 1000 mm Black/White crosses
Lower: B3 style 900 mm Black/White crosses: (Some sources specify 950 mm, others 900)
Stammkennzeichen D under starboard wing, H under port wing, originally DL   HW.

STENCILLING - Factory Standard, partially over painted

Erfolgs Tafel
Hauptmann Hahn

Lfd. Nr.	Datum	Einheit	Gegner Typ	Nationalität	Ort	Art der Vernichtung
1.	14.5.40	I./J.G.2	Hurricane	englisch	Gemblaux	brennend
2.	19.5.40	"	"	"	Tournai	abmontiert
3.	"	"	"	"	Paris	brennend
4.	3.6.40	"	"	"	Roy	"
5.	6.6.40	"	"	"	Portland	Aufschlag
6.	11.8.40	"	Spitfire	"	Dorchester	abmontiert
7.	25.8.40	"	"	"	Dover	brennend
8.	31.8.40	"	"	"	"	Aufschlag
9.	"	"	"	"	"	"
10.	"	"	"	"	Ashford	brennend
11.	4.9.40	"	Hurricane	"	Margathe	Aufschlag
12.	"	"	Spitfire	"	Ashford	"
13.	6.9.40	"	"	"	"	"
14.	"	"	"	"	Gillingham	abmontiert
15.	7.9.40	"	"	"	London	brennend
16.	8.9.40	"	Hurricane	"	Tablehurst	"
17.	11.9.40	"	"	"	Tournai	zur Landung gezwungen
18.	15.9.40	"	Spitfire	"	London	abmontiert
19.	20.9.40	"	Hurricane	"	"	Aufschlag
20.	23.9.40	"	Spitfire	"	Rochester	"
21.	15.10.40	"	"	"	Isle of Wigth	brennend
22.	6.11.40	I./J.G.2	Hurricane	"	Southampton	brennend
23.	24.6.41	"	Spitfire	"	Calais	abmontiert
24.	25.6.41	"	"	"	Marquise	Aufschlagbrand
25.	26.6.41	"	"	"	Dünkirchen	Aufschlag
26.	2.7.41	"	"	"	Hazebrouck	"
27.	7.7.41	"	Hurricane	"	Le Touquet	zerplatzt
28.	"	"	"	"	"	Aufschlag
29.	8.7.41	"	Spitfire	"	Mark	"
30.	10.7.41	"	"	"	St. Omer	brennend
31.	"	"	"	"	"	abmontiert
32.	21.7.41	"	"	"	Gravelines	"
33.	"	"	"	"	Watten	zur Landung gezwungen
34.	22.7.41	"	"	"	Calais	Aufschlag
35.	"	"	"	"	"	"
36.	23.7.41	"	"	"	Hesdin	zerplatzt
37.	"	"	"	"	"	Aufschlag
38.	5.8.41	"	"	"	Calais	"
39.	7.8.41	"	"	"	"	abmontiert
40.	12.8.41	"	"	"	Gravelines	zerplatzt
41.	"	"	"	"	Ramsgate	brennend
42.	"	"	"	"	Cap Gris Nez-Calais	abmontiert

Victory list compiled and hand written by a company clerk. It was displayed in Assi Hahn's office, it measures 12" X 24".

Personal Emblems of "Assi" Hahn

Assi Hahn's first known personal emblem. The word "Hahn" literally translated means "Rooster". Assi used this on his Bf 109 E-3 of Stab I./JG 3 "Udet", September 1939.

Assi's favorite rooster emblem used on most of his aircraft while with JG 2 "Richthofen". (Some variations are noted)

Unit Badges of "Assi" Hahn

Typical Geschwader emblem of JG 2 "Richthofen". Some versions had a White shield, Silver shield or no color in the shield. Variations in the letter "R" are known. Assi Hahn serverd in JG 2 from October 1939 to November 1942.

Badge of II. Gruppe JG 54 Grünherz (Green Hearts), the Lion of Aspern (Austria). Assi served with JG 54 from November 1942 to his capture in February 1943. During his short time as Kommandeur, the Rooster head does not appear on his aircraft.

On color profile pages, known aircraft flown by Assi Hahn designated by

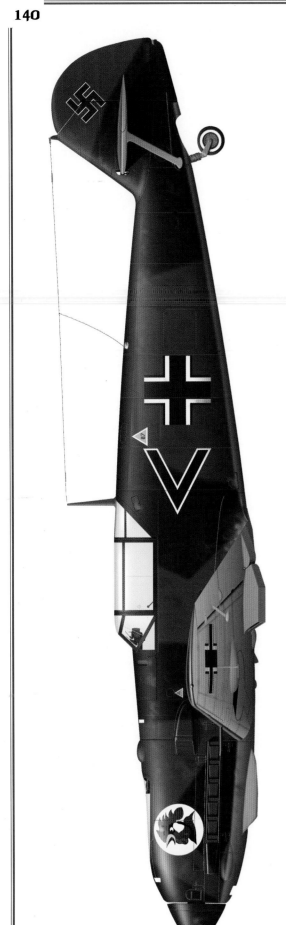

Messerschmitt Bf 109 E-3   Stab I./JG 3   September 1939   Merseburg, Germany

Aircraft No. 1

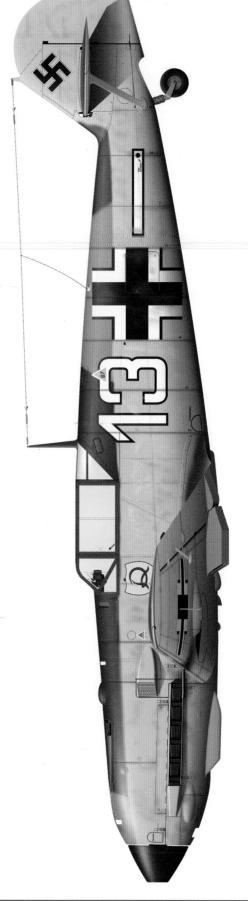

Messerschmitt Bf 109 E-3   4./JG 2   Spring 1940   Northern, Germany

Aircraft No. 2

Messerschmitt Bf 109 E-4   4./JG 2 Summer 1940 France

Aircraft No. 3

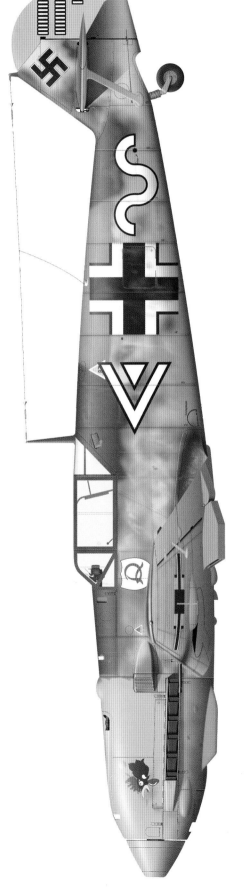

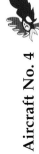

Messerschmitt Bf 109 E-4 III./JG 2   Fall 1940 Le Havre, France

Aircraft No. 4

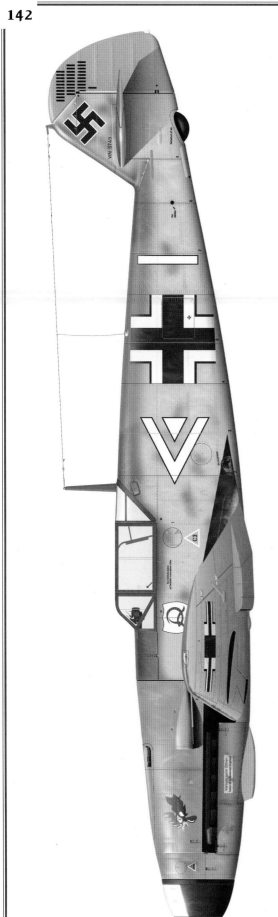

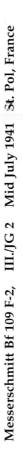

Messerschmitt Bf 109 F-2,   III./JG 2   Mid July 1941   St. Pol, France

Aircraft No. 5

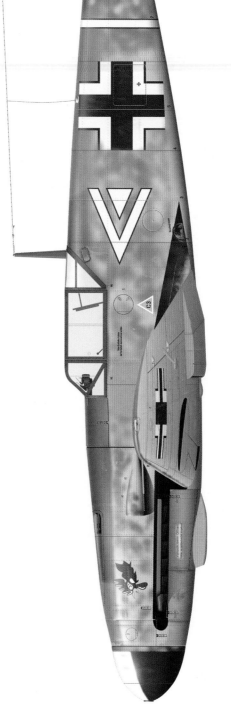

Messerschmitt Bf 109 F-2   III./JG 2   Mid July 1941   St. Pol, France

Aircraft No. 6

Messerschmitt Bf 109 F-4   III./JG 2   27 September 1941   St. Pol, France

Aircraft No. 7

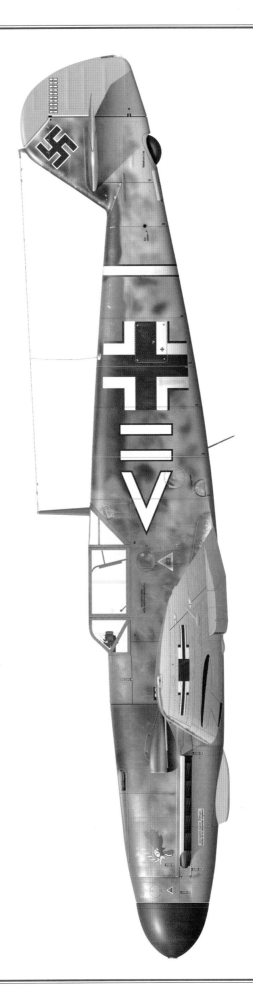

Messerschmitt Bf 109 F-4   III./JG 2   Summer 1941   St. Pol, France

Pilot: Oblt. Josef Puchinger

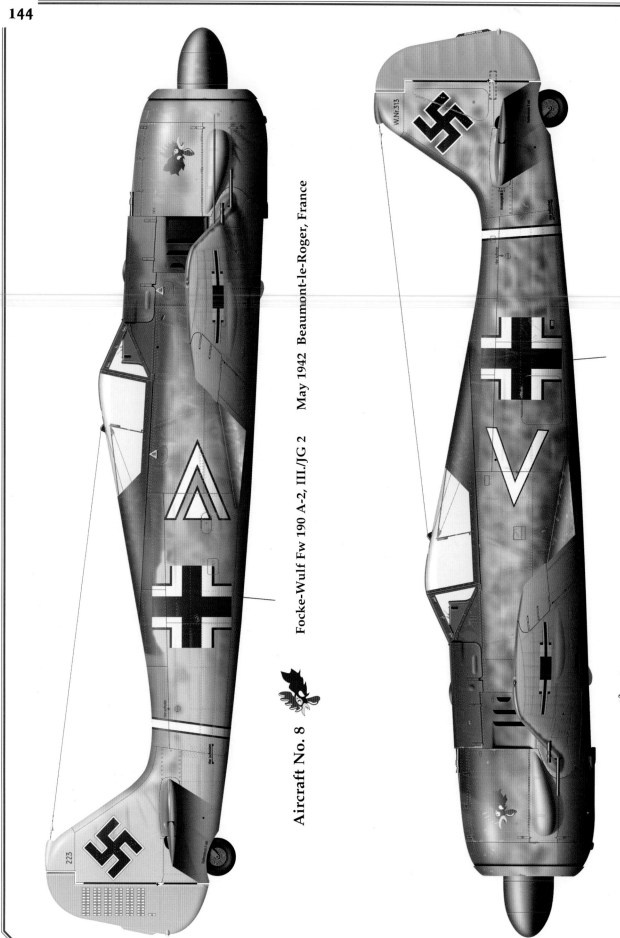

Focke-Wulf Fw 190 A-2, III./JG 2   May 1942   Beaumont-le-Roger, France

Aircraft No. 8

Focke-Wulf Fw 190 A-3, III./JG 2   May/June 1942   Cherbourg, France

Aircraft No. 9

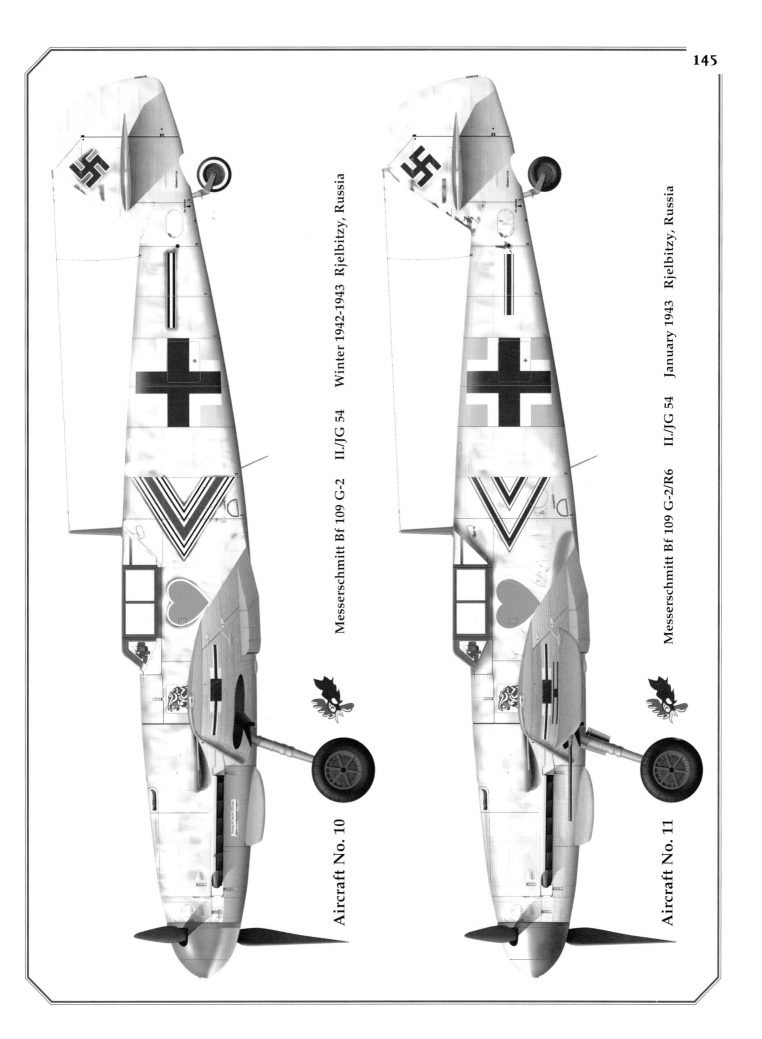

Messerschmitt Bf 109 G-2   II./JG 54   Winter 1942-1943 Rjelbitzy, Russia

Aircraft No. 10

Messerschmitt Bf 109 G-2/R6   II./JG 54   January 1943 Rjelbitzy, Russia

Aircraft No. 11

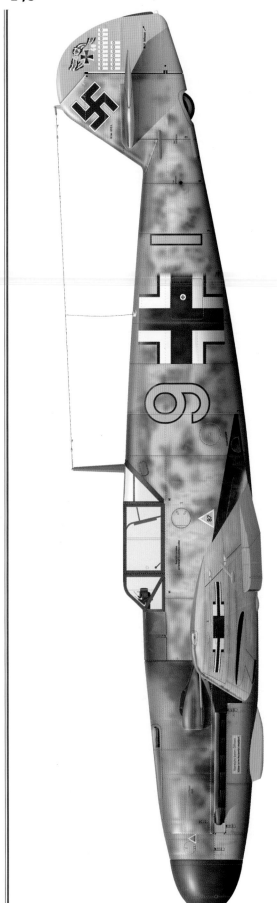

Pilot: Siegfried Schnell *Staffelkapitän* **9./JG 2**   Messerschmitt Bf 109 F-2 November 1941

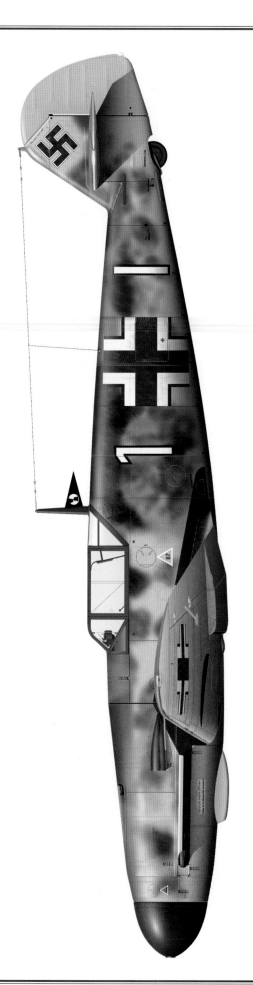

Pilot: Egon Mayer *Staffelkapitän* **7./JG 2**   Messerschmitt Bf 109 F-4 Late 1941

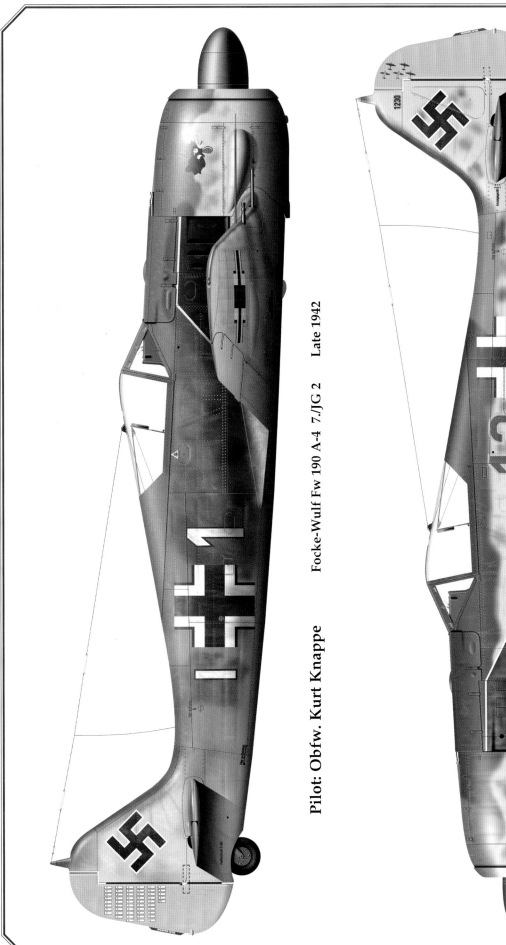

Focke-Wulf Fw 190 A-4 7./JG 2   Late 1942

Pilot: Obfw. Kurt Knappe

Focke-Wulf Fw 190 A-5   June 1943 Beaumont-le-Roger, France

Pliot: Obslt. Walter Oesau Kommodore JG 2

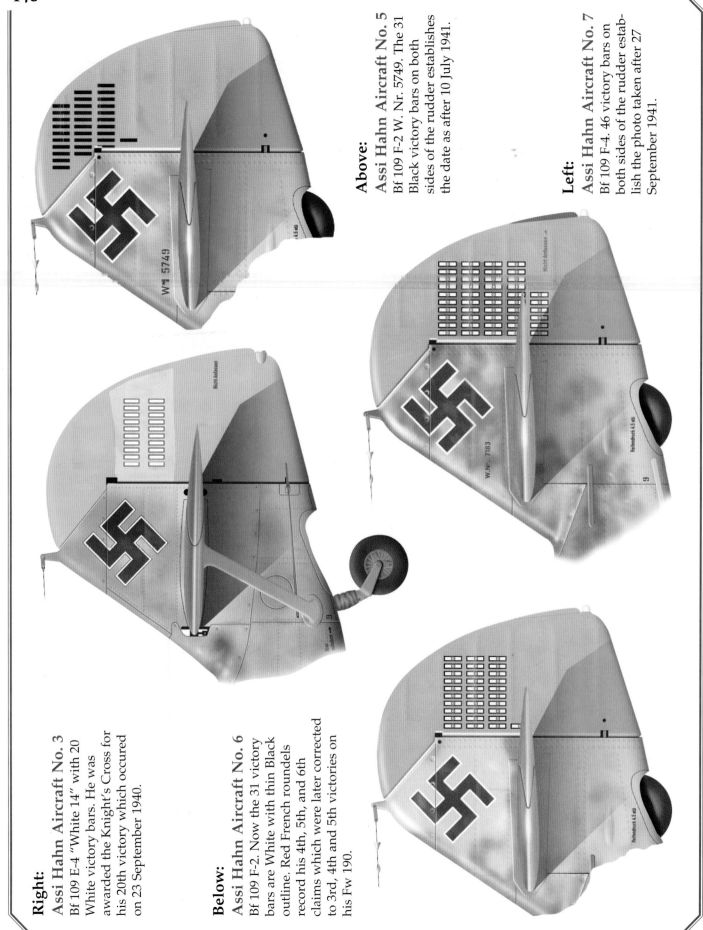

Right:
Assi Hahn Aircraft No. 3
Bf 109 E-4 "White 14" with 20 White victory bars. He was awarded the Knight's Cross for his 20th victory which occured on 23 September 1940.

Below:
Assi Hahn Aircraft No. 6
Bf 109 F-2. Now the 31 victory bars are White with thin Black outline. Red French roundels record his 4th, 5th, and 6th claims which were later corrected to 3rd, 4th and 5th victories on his Fw 190.

Above:
Assi Hahn Aircraft No. 5
Bf 109 F-2 W. Nr. 5749. The 31 Black victory bars on both sides of the rudder establishes the date as after 10 July 1941.

Left:
Assi Hahn Aircraft No. 7
Bf 109 F-4. 46 victory bars on both sides of the rudder establish the photo taken after 27 September 1941.

Right:
Walter Oesau
Fw 190 A-5 W. Nr. 1230 "Green 13" Five victories recorded as drawings of 4 engined bombers, #101 - #105, two of which show the aircraft on fire.

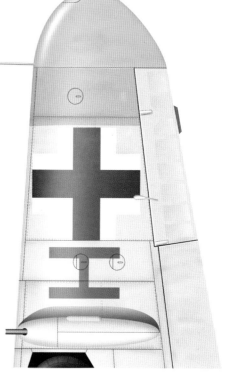

Right:
Assi Hahn Aircraft No. 8
Fw 190 A-2 W. Nr. 223. Tail scrap view shows 61 victory bars, #61 and #62 were credited on 6 May 1942, but at the time the photo was taken only a total of 61 victories were recorded. The third, fourth and fifth now reflect the correct French victories.

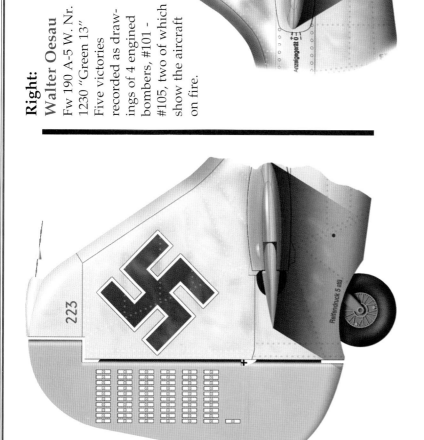

Assi Hahn Aircraft No. 11

Bf 109 G-2/R6
II./JG 54
Original
Stammkennzeichen
DL HW.
"D" on starboard and "W" on port wing overpainted by Yellow underwing tips.

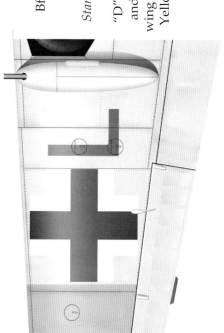

Aircraft flown by Assi Hahn but not his personal machines.

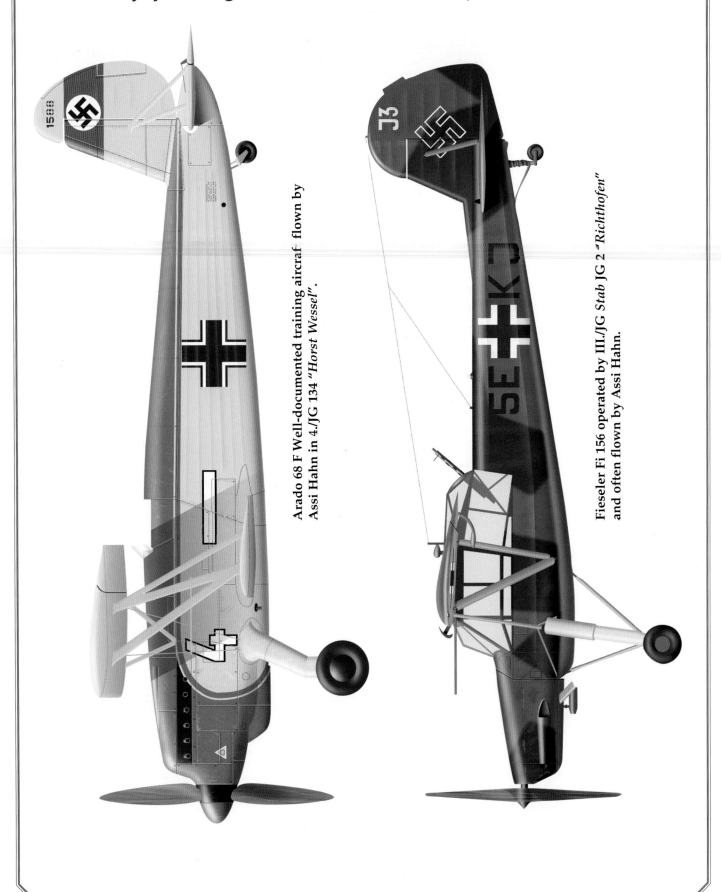

Arado 68 F Well-documented training aircraf flown by
Assi Hahn in 4./JG 134 "Horst Wessel".

Fieseler Fi 156 operated by III./JG Stab JG 2 "Richthofen"
and often flown by Assi Hahn.

This Agfa color film was shot in July 1941 at St. Pol, France. The quality is not the best but is presented due to its rarity.

Checking under the hood of Assi's staff car.

Egon Mayer on the left looking at Assi's newly-presented victory stick.

*An unidentified **Luftwaffe** officer shaking the paw of Lux, Assi's Harlequin Great Dane. This officer does not appear to be a pilot as he is not wearing **Luftwaffe** pilot's wings.*

An nice color photo taken from inside the Chateau at St. Pol, France.

Next page; a colorized photo of Assi Hahn with Icko, his pet donkey. St. Pol, France

The enchanting Gisela Hahn in front of a
war-time oil portrait of Assi Hahn.

Gisela Hahn sitting in Doug Champlin's converted Spanish "Buchon"
which is painted in the markings of Assi Hahn's Bf 109. Photo taken during
a Fighter Aces symposium at the Champlin Museum in 1990.

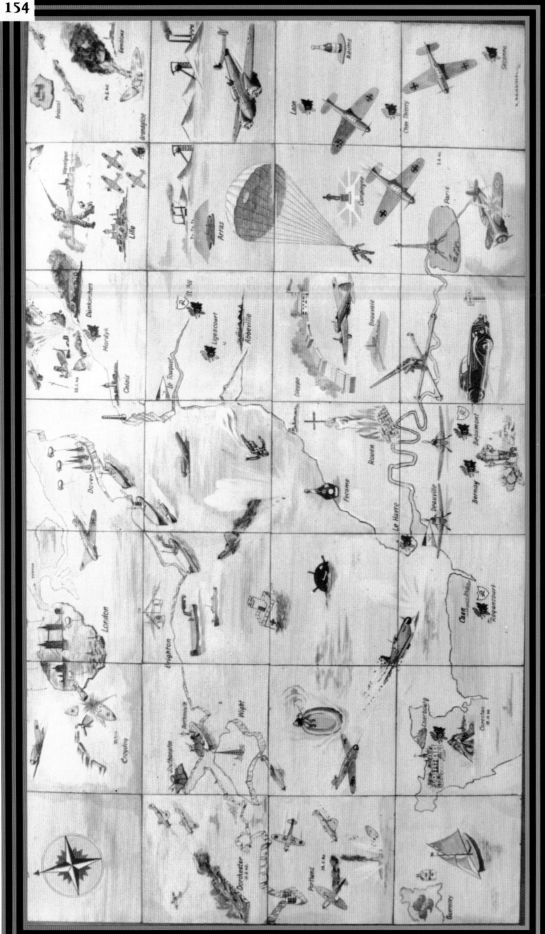

A special table commissioned by Hans "Assi" Hahn consisting of hand-painted tiles by H. Relcksiegel in 1941, details Assi's victories and the highlights of his early Luftwaffe career. His first victory is recorded on 14 May 1940 over a Hurricane near Gemblaux Belgium, upper right. Missions over Dunkerque, 28 May 1940, are illustrated center top. His fourth victory on 3 June 1940 over a French P-36 can be seen on the bottom right. At left center is his 6th victory on 11 August 1940 over a Spitfire. The 7th victory

which occured on 25 August 1940 over a Spitfire can be seen in the center left. On the table it is listed as Fortland England however on the victory board it is listed as Dover. The last illustrated victory is 23 September 1940 when a Spitfire exploded over Croyden, which is his 20th can be seen on the top left. This unique commemorative piece of furniture was requested by Assi with the order for the artist to be 'locked in the room until the painting is finished'.

Commemorative Tile Table of "Assi" Hahn

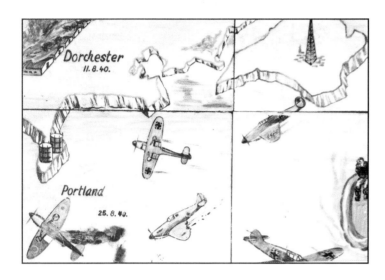

The left side portion of the table illustrating an air battle on 25 August 1940 when Assi shot down a Spitfire, labeled on the table as Portland but listed as dover on his personal victory board, see page 138. The Bf 109s are illustrated as F types with Yellow undercowls.

Below: Close up of the lower center, his Rooster emblem indicates areas of interest on the French coast where Assi was involved. The "Richthofen" emblem locates JG 2 air bases.

Below: Detailed image below shows the upper right hand corner indicating the **Stab** based at Le Touquet, Assi's unit at St. Pol, Dunkerque, and Assi goose hunting. Upper right is the area of Assi's first victory in Belgium on 14 May 1940 where he claimed two Hurricanes but was officially credited with just one.

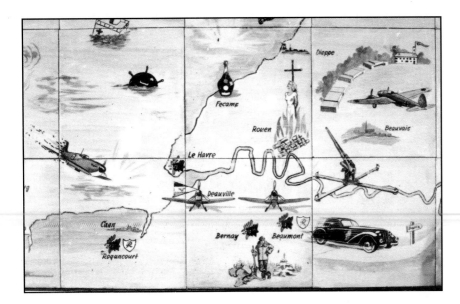

Left: Lower center of tile table showing detail of JG 2 near Rogancourt and Beaumont-le-Roger and Assi successfully hunting a stag, see page 48 where the antlers from the hunt are displayed on the Gefechtsstand. Note also the detailed image of his racy, black sportscar.

Right: Note the illustration of his victory over a French P-36 on 3 June 1940. The signature of the artist, H. Relksiegel, 1941, can also be seen in the lower right hand corner.

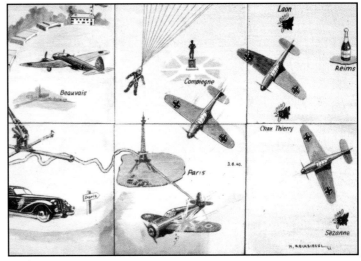

Below: Overall view of this historic, commemorative table.

Chapter Eleven

Documents & Victory List

Menu for a party held in Richthofen Staffel

Im Namen des Reichs

ernenne ich den Oberfähnrich
                H a n s   H a h n
bei den Offizieren z.b.V. des Reichsministers der Luftfahrt (Schüleretat)
          mit Wirkung vom 1. April 1936 zum
                 L e u t n a n t
     mit einem Rangdienstalter vom 1. April 1936 (297).

    Ich vollziehe diese Urkunde in der Erwartung, daß der Ernannte getreu seinem Diensteide, seine Berufspflichten gewissenhaft erfüllt und das Vertrauen rechtfertigt, das ihm durch diese Ernennung bewiesen wird.
    Zugleich darf er des besonderen Schutzes des Führers und Reichskanzlers sicher sein.

                Berlin, den 20. April 1936.
        Namens des Führers und Reichskanzlers
          Der Reichsminister der Luftfahrt
        und Oberbefehlshaber der Luftwaffe.

Promotion certificate from Oberfähnrich *to* Leutnant *1 April 1936.*

Im Namen des Führers und Reichskanzlers

befördere ich

den Leutnant in der Luftwaffe

H a n s   H a h n

mit Wirkung vom 1. Februar 1939 zum

O b e r l e u t n a n t

Ich vollziehe diese Urkunde in der Erwartung, daß der Genannte getreu seinem Diensteide seine Berufspflichten gewissenhaft erfüllt und das Vertrauen rechtfertigt, das ihm durch diese Beförderung bewiesen wird. Zugleich darf er des besonderen Schutzes des Führers und Reichskanzlers sicher sein.

Berlin, den   20. Januar 1939.

Der Reichsminister der Luftfahrt und Oberbefehlshaber der Luftwaffe

Promotion certificate from Leutnant to Oberleutnant 1 February 1939

Verleihungsurkunde

Im Namen des
Oberbefehlshabers der Luftwaffe

verleihe ich dem

Hauptmann Hans　H a h n

III./Jagdgeschwader Richthofen Nr. 2

die

Frontflug-Spange für Jäger

in Gold

Gefechtsstand　　　,den　26. 4. 194 1

Hauptmann u. Geschwaderkommodore

Award document for combat flying clasp in gold presented after 110 combat missions.

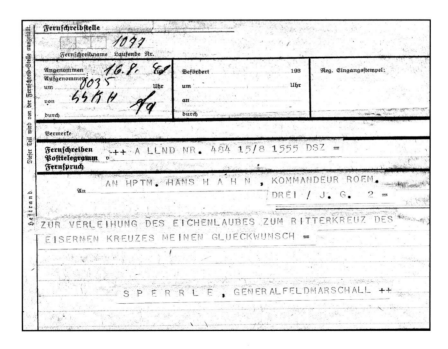

Message: *My most cordial congratulations for your award of the Oak Leaves to the Knights Cross of the Iron Cross.*

Erhard Milch,
Generalfeldmarschall

Messsage:

To *Hauptmann Hans Hahn, Kommandeur III. / JG 2*

My congratulations on the occasion of your award of the Oak Leaves to the Ritterkreuz.

Sperrle,
Generalfeldmarschall

Fernschreibstelle **J.G. 2**   **Geheim**

L **L E P** 01015   ~~Geheime Kommandosache~~
Fernschreibname Laufende Nr.

~~~~~~~~
Aufgenommen

Datum: **14. August** 19**41**

um: **22.10** Uhr

von: **LL AO**

durch: **Re.**

Befördert:

Datum: 19

um: Uhr

an:

durch:

Rolle:

Vermerke:

Fernschreiben
Posttelegramm von + KR GLBKW NR 0575   14/8   1945   DSZ=
Fernspruch

| Abgangstag | Abgangszeit | An HERRN HAUPTMANN HAHN |
| | | ROEM DREI / J.G. 2 UEBER LFL. KDO. 3.= |

--- G E H E I M ---
Vermerke für Beförderung (vom Aufgeber auszufüllen)   Bestimmungsort

IN DANKBARER WUERDIGUNG IHRES HELDENHAFTEN EINSATZES

IM KAMPF FUER DIE ZUKUNFT UNSERES VOLKES VERLEIHE

ICH IHNEN ANLAESZLICH IHRES 42. LUFTSIEGES ALS

32. OFFIZIER DER DEUTSCHEN WEHRMACHT DAS EICHENLAUB

ZUM RITTERKREUZ DES EISERNEN KREUZES.=

(GEZ) ADOLF HITLER.

OB.D!L. FUEHR.STAB. ROEM EINS NR. 30920/41 geh (B 1)++

Message: In grateful acknowledgment of your heroic engagement in the battle for the future of our people, I convey to you Oak Leaves to the Knight's Cross of the Iron Cross on the occasion of your 42nd aerial victory as the 32nd officer of the German **Wehrmacht.**

(signed) Adolf Hitler

Hans "Assi" Hahn
Officially Credited Victory List

4./JG 2

Number	Date	Aircraft Type	Time
1.	14 May 1940	Hurricane	09:55
2.	19 May 1940	Hurricane	12:18
3.	19 May 1940	Morane	--
4.	3 June 1940	P-36	14:50
5.	6 June 1940	Morane	20:35
6.	11 August 1940	Spitfire	11:45
7.	25 August 1940	Spitfire	--
8.	31 August 1940	Spitfire	09:00
9.	31 August 1940	Spitfire	09:05
10.	31 August 1940	Spitfire	19:05
11.	4 September 1940	Spitfire[1]	10:15
12.	4 September 1940	Spitfire	14:25
13.	6 September 1940	Spitfire	10:00
14.	6 September 1940	Spitfire	10:05
15.	7 September 1940	Spitfire	18:25
16.	8 September 1940	Hurricane	--
17.	11 September 1940	Hurricane	16:15
18.	15 September 1940	Spitfire	15:35
19.	20 September 1940	Hurricane	12:15
20.	23 September 1940	Spitfire	10:30
21.	15 October 1940	Hurricane[2]	13:35

III./JG 2

Number	Date	Aircraft Type	Time
22.	6 November 1940	Hurricane	15:55
23.	24 June 1941	Spitfire	21:00
24.	25 June 1941	Spitfire	16:31
25.	26 June 1941	Spitfire	11:55
26.	2 July 1941	Hurricane	--
27.	7 July 1941	Hurricane	15:36
28.	7 July 1941	Spitfire	15:37
29.	8 July 1941	Spitfire	15:52
30.	10 July 1941	Spitfire	12:08

Number	Date	Aircraft Type	Time
31.	10 July 1941	Spitfire	12:12
32.	21 July 1941	Spitfire	08:50
33.	21 July 1941	Spitfire	20:45
34.	22 July 1941	Spitfire	13:45
35.	22 July 1941	Spitfire	13:53
36.	23 July 1941	Spitfire	20:20
37.	23 July 1941	Spitfire	20:23
38.	5 August 1941	Spitfire	18:44
39.	7 August 1941	Spitfire	18:17
40.	12 August 1941	Spitfire	12:45
41.	12 August 1941	Spitfire	12:50
42.	12 August 1941	Spitfire	18:51
43.	20 September 1941	Spitfire	16:30
44.	20 September 1941	Spitfire	16:42
45.	20 September 1941	Spitfire	16:43
46.	27 September 1941	Spitfire	15:35
47.	2 October 1941	Spitfire	15:05
48.	2 October 1941	Spitfire	18:50
49.	2 October 1941	Spitfire	18:52
50.	13 October 1941	Spitfire	14:30
51.	12 February 1942	Spitfire	14:55
52.	17 April 1942	Spitfire	16:08
53.	20 April 1942	Spitfire	17:07
54.	22 April 1942	Spitfire	17:07
55.	25 April 1942	Spitfire	16:24
56.	25 April 1942	Spitfire	16:29
57.	30 April 1942	Spitfire	17:27
58.	4 May 1942	Spitfire	10:41
59.	4 May 1942	Spitfire	10:46
60.	4 May 1942	Spitfire	15:55
61.	6 May 1942	Spitfire	12:22
62.	6 May 1942	Spitfire	12:24
63.	6 June 1942	Spitfire	17:25
64.	6 June 1942	Spitfire	17:25
65.	6 June 1942	Spitfire	17:27
66.	16 September 1942	Spitfire	13:15

II./JG 54

Number	Date	Aircraft Type	Time
67.	4 December 1942	Lagg 3	10:45
68.	4 December 1942	Il-2	10:47
69.	4 December 1942	Il-2	13:53
70.	4 December 1942	Il-2	14:00

Number	Date	Aircraft Type	Time
71.	12 December 1942	La-5	13:56
72.	12 December 1942	Il-2	13:58
73.	29 December 1942	Il-2	11:30
74.	29 December 1942	Lagg 3	11:50
75.	30 December 1942	Lagg 3	08:50
76.	30 December 1942	Lagg 3	08:53
77.	30 December 1942	Lagg 3	08:55
78.	30 December 1942	Il-2	08:57
79.	30 December 1942	Lagg 3	11:45
80.	14 January 1943	La 5	10:36
81.	14 January 1943	La 5	10:37
82.	14 January 1943	La 5	10:38
83.	14 January 1943	La 5	10:42
84.	14 January 1943	La 5	12:10
85.	14 January 1943	La 5	12:11
86.	14 January 1943	La 5	12:12
87.	23 January 1943	La 5	13:20
88.	23 January 1943	La 5	13:22
89.	23 January 1943	La 5	13:25
90.	24 January 1943	La 5	09:35
91.	24 January 1943	La 5	09:40
92.	24 January 1943	La 5	09:42
93.	24 January 1943	La 5	13:55
94.	25 January 1943	La 5	09:45
95.	25 January 1943	La 5	09:47
96.	25 January 1943	Lagg 3	09:48
97.	26 January 1943	Lagg 3	10:58
98.	26 January 1943	Lagg 3	14:00
99.	26 January 1943	Lagg 3	14:03
100.	27 January 1943	Lagg 3	10:43
101.	8 February 1943	unknown	
102.	9 February 1943	P-40	13:10
103.	9 February 1943	P-40	13:11
104.	11 February 1943	P-40	09:52
105.	11 February 1943	P-40	09:58
106.	11 February 1943	Lagg 3	10:08
107.	11 February 1943	Il-2	11:30
108.	21 February 1943	La 5	09:11 (09:09?)

Document supplied by Hans Ring

Chapter 11 Notes:

1. Some records indicate Hurricane   2. Some records indicate Spitfire

Selected Bibliography

Frappe, Jean-Bernard. *La Luftwaffe Attaque a L'Ouest*, (France 1939-1942), Editions Heimdal. France.

Mombeek, Eric. *Luftwaffe Colours Volume One Section 4 Jagdwaffe, Attack in the West, May 1940,* Classic Publications Ltd. England, 2000.

Nauroth, Holger. *Jagdgeschwader 2 "Richthofen"*, Motorbuch Verlag. Germany, 1999.

Obermierer, Ernst. *Die Ritterkreuzträger der Luftwaffe 1939-1945.* Verlag Dieter Hoffmann. Germany 1989.

Prien, Jochen; Stemmer, Gerhard; Bock, Winfried. *Die Jagdfliegerverbände der Deutschen Luftwaffe 1934 bis 1945. Tiel 2 Der Sitzkrieg 1.9.1939 bis 9.5.1940.* Struve-Druck. Germany.

Prien, Jochen; Rodeike, Peter. *Messerschmitt Bf 109 F, G, & K Series.* Schiffer, USA, 1993.

Ries, Karl. *Dora Kurfürst und rote 13.* Verlag Dieter Hoffmann. Germany, 1964.

Rodeike, Peter. *Focke-Wulf Jagdflugzeug Fw 190 A, Fw 190 "Dora", Ta 152 H.* Struve-Druck. Germany.

Weal, John. *Jagdgeschwader 2 "Richthofen".* Osprey Publishing. England 2000.

Sources and Interview Notes

Messerschmitt factory diagrams for camouflage and markings 8-109 G.a Messerschmitt A.G. Augsburg, Germany, 1941.

Diethelm von Eichel-Strieber: Knight's Cross holder, 96 victories scored while serving in several different units including JG 2, JG 5, JG 26, JG 27, JG 51, JG 52 and JG 77. Author conducted numerous interviews on tape, in correspondence and personal visits, through the years from 1970 to his death in 1996. Diet flew with Assi Hahn, Egon Mayer and other members of JG 2 in July 1941. His memory was vivid and accurate.

Erich Hartmann: world's highest scoring fighter pilot with 352 credited victories. The author's first contact with Hartmann, through correspondence, began in 1968 and continued in person at his home in Germany over the years. One of his first comments about *Luftwaffe* fighter pilots was about Assi Hahn's skill and honor.

Adolf Galland: former *General der Jagdflieger*, author's friendship began in 1980. The *General* kindly granted many discussions and interviews during many meetings both in his home in Germany and at various functions around the world until his death in February 1996.

Julius Meimberg: life-long friend and wingman to Assi Hahn from their first days in 4./JG 2. Assi shared details and stories with *Herr* Meimberg as to no one else. Author conducted several interviews with *Herr* Meimberg both on tape and correspondence.

Hannes Trautloft: Assi and the late *General* Trautloft were classmates in war college in München together in 1935. Then, Trautloft as *Geschwaderkommodore* of JG 54 requested Assi for the job of II./JG 54 *Gruppenkommandeur* to take over for Dieter Hrabak who was transferred to take command of JG 52. *General* Trautloft had only good things to say about Assi as a soldier during the several interviews at his home in München and in Baden-Baden with the author.

Many other interviews with family and friends including Helga von Hols who knew Assi very well.